HAL LEONARD

Pocket Piano Chord Dictionary

by Andrew DuBrock

ISBN 978-1-4234-8436-3

HAL•LEONARD®
7777 W. BLUEMOUND RD. P.O. BOX 13819 MILWAUKEE, WI 53213

Contact Us:
Hal Leonard
7777 West Bluemound Road
Milwaukee, WI 53213
Email: info@halleonard.com

In Australia contact:
Hal Leonard Australia Pty. Ltd.
4 Lentara Court
Cheltenham, Victoria, 3192 Australia
Email: ausadmin@halleonard.com.a

In Europe contact:
Hal Leonard Europe Limited
42 Wigmore Street
Marylebone, London, W1U 2RN
Email: info@halleonardeurope.com

Visit Hal Leonard Online at
www.halleonard.com

Table of Contents

Introduction

The *Pocket Piano Chord Dictionary* is an extensive reference guide to over 1,300 chords. Forty-two different chord qualities are covered for each key, and most chord qualities are presented in multiple different voicings. When a chord is complete in both the treble and bass clef notation, the two staves are not connected. If a chord's voicing is spread between the treble and bass clefs the staves are connected. For ease of readability, all sharp/flat chord names are labeled with the letter having the fewest accidentals in its key signature (i.e. D♭ instead of C♯, since D♭ has five flats and C♯ has seven sharps). The enharmonic sharp or flat name can be substituted, and is listed at the top of each page.

No book would be long enough to include every possible voicing for each chord type. However, this dictionary gives you the tools to build your own voicings, enabling you to create every possible voicing yourself (see *Using the Dictionary to Build Chord Voicings* on page 10).

To increase the number of voicings in this book, different letter names may have different voicings for the same chord type and also may include different inversions of the chord (see *Inversions* in the *Chord Construction* section for more on this). If you like a particular Cmaj7 voicing, for instance, you can always transfer that voicing to Dmaj7 or any other root. Keep in mind that different chord types may share the same notes (see the *Chord Construction* section for an explanation).

Chord Construction

You don't need to know theory to play music, but it can help you understand the music you play better. If you'd like to learn more about chord construction theory, read on!

Triads

Triad is a Greek word that means "three," and that's exactly what a triad contains—three notes! Triads are the most common type of chord. They are built by stacking two thirds on top of each other. When we say "thirds," we're talking about intervals—the distance between notes. If you start on one note and move up the scale, the distance between the first note and the next note is a *2nd*. The distance between the first note and the third note is a *3rd*, between the first and fourth is a *4th*, and so on. Thirds can be either major or minor, and stacking these thirds on top of each other in different combinations creates four types of triads: major, minor, diminished, and augmented. Here is what's known as a C Major triad:

root   third   fifth

The defining note of a chord (its letter name) is called the *root*. Notice how the second note in the triad is the third. The top note is called the 5th because its interval with the root is a 5th (count up yourself to see). After we take a closer look at intervals, we'll look at the different types of triads you can build with those intervals. So, continue on for more on triads.

Intervals

The *triad* section briefly discussed what an interval is: the distance between any two notes. Counting up from the first note to the second note will give you the interval between those two notes. That distance is quantified with a number, but intervals also have another component: their *quality*. The quality of any interval can be major, minor, diminished, augmented, or perfect. Looking at the twelve notes in a chromatic scale, along with their intervals, can help explain the differences between these qualities:

You may notice that every minor interval is one half step smaller than its major-interval counterpart. The only intervals that are not major or minor are the *perfect* intervals–the 4th and 5th. Lowering a perfect interval (like the fourth) results in a diminished interval, while raising a perfect interval (like the fifth) results in an augmented interval. All the other non-perfect intervals can be diminished or augmented as well, though it rarely happens. Here's how: if you lower a minor interval by one half step, it becomes diminished; and if you raise a major interval by one half step, it becomes augmented.

Now let's look at all the different types of triads we can build with these intervals. There are four types: major, minor, diminished, and augmented. Major triads have a major 3rd and a perfect 5th;

minor triads have a minor third and a perfect 5th; diminished triads have a minor third and a diminished fifth; and augmented triads have a major third and an augmented fifth:

Major triads are labeled with just a letter (C, above), minor triads are labeled with a lowercase "m" (Cm, above), diminished triads are labeled with a "°" (C°), and augmented chords are labeled with a "+" (C+).

7th Chords

Seventh chords are four-note chords that stack a 7th interval on top of a triad. There are four types of unaltered 7th chords: dominant 7th (labeled with a "7" after the chord's letter name), minor seventh (m7), major seventh (maj7), and minor-major 7th [m(maj7)]. Here are the 7th chords with a C root:

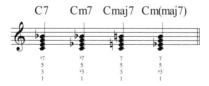

Extended Chords

Beyond 7th chords, you can add further extensions to color the chord even more. Basically, you continue stacking 3rds on top of a 7th chord to build extended chords. Stack one third on top and you have a 9th chord, add a 3rd to the 9th chord and you have an 11th chord, and add a 3rd to that 11th chord to get a 13th chord.

Not all notes of an extended chord are necessary to complete the chord, but some of the notes are more important to include than others. For a chord to be an extended chord, you have to include the 7th and the extension. After that, including the third, root, and other extensions hold lesser priority. The least important note to include in an extended chord is the 5th.

Dominant 11th chords typically omit the 3rd, and dominant 13 and maj13 chords typically omit the 11th (which conflicts with the 3rd).

It's also important to note that extensions can appear in a different octave than their numerical name implies. For instance, a 13th down one octave is a 6th. You can use that 6th (instead of a 13th) in your chord and it will still be considered a 13th chord as long as you have a 7th in the chord, as well.

Suspended, "Add," and Other Chords

Suspended chords (sus) are formed when a note is substituted for a chord tone. In a sus4 chord, for instance, the 4th is substituted for the 3rd. "Add" chords are simply chords that add one or several notes to any particular chord. The difference between a sus4 and an add4 chord is that the sus4 does not include the 3rd, while the add4 does. Of course, like the English language, there are always a few exceptions. A triad with an added 6th is simply a 6th chord (though it could be written as an add6 chord), and a chord with the 6th and 9th added is simply called a "six-nine chord" ($^6_9$).

Altered Chords

Any chord can be altered, and that alteration is reflected in the chord's name. For instance, if you alter a 7th chord by lowering the 5th one half step, you have a 7♭5 chord; raise the 5th of that 7th chord by one half step, and you have a 7♯5 chord.

Inversions

Some of the chords in this book are voiced in inversion. Any time that the lowest note in a chord is not the root, then the chord is in inversion. The more notes you have in a chord, the more possible inversions you have. For instance, a 7th chord can be played in more inversions than a triad.

Same Shapes, Different Names

Many chords can be called more than one name. For instance, a ♭5th is equivalent to a ♯11, and a chord containing one of these notes could be labeled either way. Likewise, a ♯5th and a ♭13th are also equivalent. Keep this in mind if you're unable to find the chord type you're looking for; you may find it by looking up its enharmonic equivalent.

Using the Dictionary to Build Chord Voicings

No dictionary would be large enough to include every voicing for every chord type, but by understanding how each chord is built, you *can* come up with any possible voicing on your own.

Each chord quality in this book is built from a formula. Those formulas are shown on pages 11-12 for all of the chords in this book and the formulas are repeated throughout the book next to each chord quality they apply to. Using these formulas, you can build any possible voicing for any chord type. For instance, after the "Major" chords heading on page 13, you'll see the major chord formula in brackets [R–3–5]. Using those scale degrees—the root, 3rd, and 5th—you can build a major chord anywhere on the keyboard. Below each voicing in the book, the diagrams illustrate which notes correspond to which of the formula's scale degrees. For instance, in the first voicing on page 13, under the notes C, E, and G, you'll see the scale degrees R, 3, and 5, respectively. Once you know which notes correspond to which scale degrees, you can put the notes of that formula together in any place on the keyboard, and in any inversion (If you are unfamiliar with the formulas, read the *Chord Construction* section on page 5.)

Chord Qualities

Following is a list of the forty-two chord qualities presented in this book, their abbreviations, and their formulas. Some of the extended chords omit one or more notes (see the *chord construction* section for more information on this).

CHORD TYPE	ABBREVIATION	FORMULA
Major	C	1–3–5
Minor	Cm	1–♭3–5
Diminished	C°	1–♭3–♭5
Augmented	C+	1–3–♯5
Dominant Seventh	C7	1–3–5–♭7
Seventh, Flat Fifth	C7♭5	1–3–♭5–♭7
Seventh, Sharp Fifth	C7♯5	1–3–♯5–♭7
Seventh, Flat Ninth	C7♭9	1–3–5–♭7–♭9
Seventh, Sharp Ninth	C7♯9	1–3–5–♭7–♯9
Seventh, Flat Ninth, Flat Fifth	C7♭9♭5	1–3–♭5–♭7–♭9
Seventh, Flat Ninth, Sharp Fifth	C7♭9♯5	1–3–♯5–♭7–♭9
Seventh, Sharp Ninth, Flat Fifth	C7♯9♭5	1–3–♭5–♭7–♯9
Seventh, Sharp Ninth, Sharp Fifth	C7♯9♯5	1–3–♯5–♭7–♯9
Major Seventh	Cmaj7	1–3–5–7
Major Seventh, Flat Fifth	Cmaj7♭5	1–3–♭5–7
Major Seventh, Sharp Fifth	Cmaj7♯5	1–3–♯5–7
Minor Seventh	Cm7	1–♭3–5–♭7
Minor Seventh, Flat Fifth	Cm7♭5	1–♭3–♭5–♭7
Minor, Major Seventh	Cm(maj7)	1–♭3–5–7
Diminished Seventh	C°7	1–♭3–♭5–♭♭7
Ninth	C9	1–3–5–♭7–9
Ninth, Sharp Fifth	C9♯5	1–3–♯5–♭7–9
Major Ninth	Cmaj9	1–3–5–7–9
Minor Ninth	Cm9	1–♭3–5–♭7–9
Minor, Major Ninth	Cm(maj9)	1–♭3–5–7–9
Eleventh	C11	1–3–5–♭7–9–11
Minor Eleventh	Cm11	1–♭3–5–♭7–9–11
Thirteenth	C13	1–3–5–♭7–9–13

CHORD TYPE	ABBREVIATION	FORMULA
Major Thirteenth	Cmaj13	1–3–5–7–9–13
Minor Thirteenth	Cm13	1–♭3–5–♭7–9–11–13
Sixth	C6	1–3–5–6
Six-Nine	C$^6_9$	1–3–5–6–9
Minor Sixth	Cm6	1–♭3–5–6
Minor Six-Nine	Cm$^6_9$	1–♭3–5–6–9
Fifth (Power Chord)	C5	1–5
Suspended Second	Csus2	1–2–5
Suspended Fourth	Csus4	1–4–5
Seventh, Suspended Fourth	C7sus4	1–4–5–♭7
Ninth, Suspended Fourth	C9sus4	1–4–5–♭7–9
Add Fourth	Cadd4	1–3–4–5
Add Ninth	Cadd9	1–3–5–9
Minor, Add Ninth	Cm(add9)	1–♭3–5–9

C

Triads

Major [R–3–5]

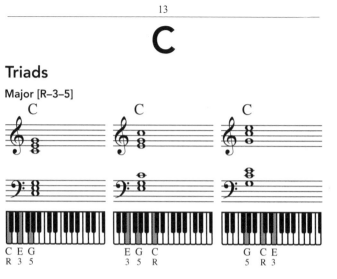

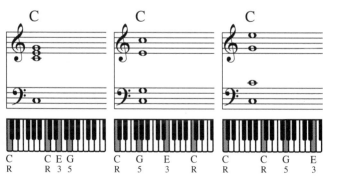

C

Minor (m, -) [R–♭3–5]

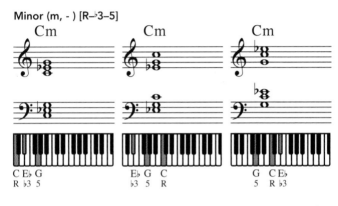

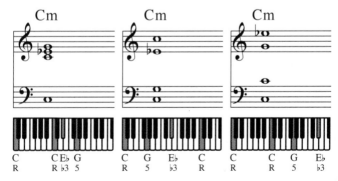

C

Diminished (°, dim) [R–♭3–♭5]

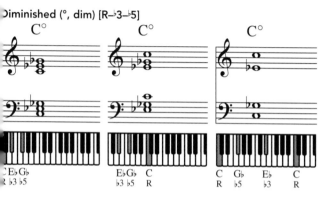

Augmented (+, aug) [R–3–♯5]

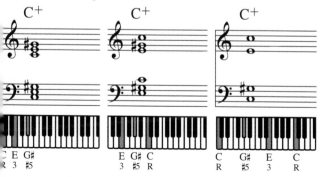

C

Seventh Chords

Dominant Seventh (7) [R–3–5–♭7]

C7

C7

C7

C E G B♭
R 3 5 ♭7

E G B♭ C
3 5 ♭7 R

G B♭ C E
5 ♭7 R 3

C7

C7

C7

B♭ C E G
♭7 R 3 5

C G E B♭
R 5 3 ♭7

C B♭ G E
R ♭7 5 3

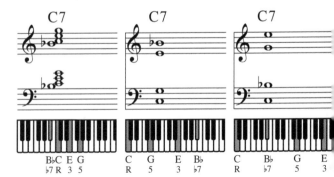

C

Dominant Seventh Chords with Alterations

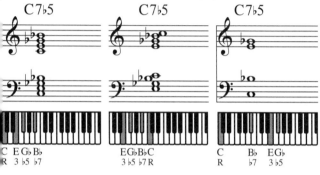

C7♭5

C E G♭ B♭
R 3 ♭5 ♭7

C7♭5

E G♭ B♭ C
3 ♭5 ♭7 R

C7♭5

C   B♭   E G♭
R   ♭7   3 ♭5

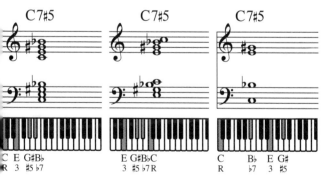

C7♯5

C E G♯ B♭
R 3 ♯5 ♭7

C7♯5

E G♯ B♭ C
3 ♯5 ♭7 R

C7♯5

C   B♭   E G♯
R   ♭7   3 ♯5

C

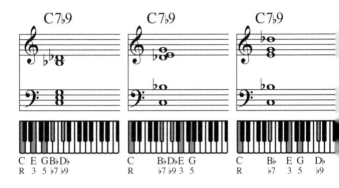

C7♭9   C7♭9   C7♭9

C E G B♭ D♭	C B♭ D♭ E G	C B♭ E G D♭
R 3 5 ♭7 ♭9	R ♭7 ♭9 3 5	R ♭7 3 5 ♭9

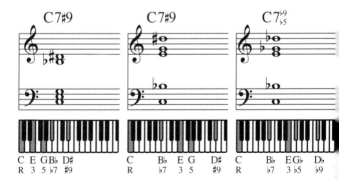

C7#9   C7#9   C7♭9♭5

C E G B♭ D#	C B♭ E G D#	C B♭ E♭ D♭
R 3 5 ♭7 #9	R ♭7 3 5 #9	R ♭7 3 ♭5 ♭9

C

$C7^{\flat 9}_{\sharp 5}$

B♭	D♭	E	G♯
♭7	♭9	3	♯5
R			

$C7^{\sharp 9}_{\flat 5}$

C	B♭	E	G♭	D♯
R	♭7	3	♭5	♯9

$C7^{\sharp 9}_{\sharp 5}$

C	B♭	E	G♯	D♯
R	♭7	3	♯5	♯9

Major Seventh (maj7, M7, ma7, 7) [R–3–5–7]

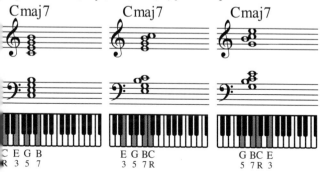

Cmaj7

C	E	G	B
R	3	5	7

Cmaj7

E	G	B	C
3	5	7	R

Cmaj7

G	B	C	E
5	7	R	3

C

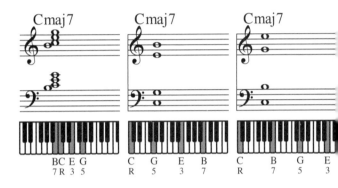

Cmaj7	Cmaj7	Cmaj7
BC E G 7 R 3 5	C G E B R 5 3 7	C B G E R 7 5 3

Major Seventh Chords with Alterations

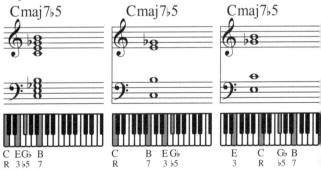

Cmaj7♭5	Cmaj7♭5	Cmaj7♭5
C EG♭ B R 3♭5 7	C B EG♭ R 7 3♭5	E C G♭ B 3 R ♭5 7

C

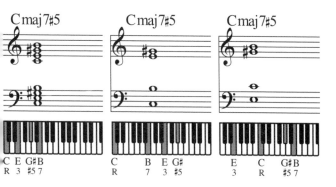

Cmaj7#5   Cmaj7#5   Cmaj7#5

C E G#B   C   B E G#   E   C   G#B
R 3 #5 7   R   7 3 #5   3   R   #5 7

Minor Seventh (m7, min7, -7) [R–♭3–5–♭7]

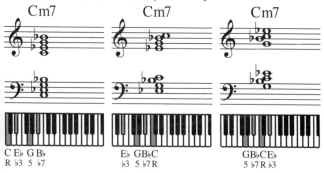

Cm7   Cm7   Cm7

C E♭ G B♭   E♭ G B♭ C   G B♭ C E♭
R ♭3 5 ♭7   ♭3 5 ♭7 R   5 ♭7 R ♭3

C

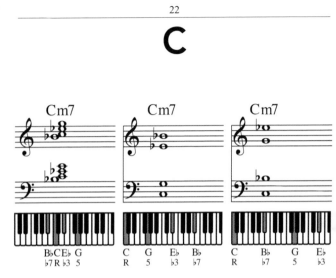

Cm7
B♭CE♭ G
♭7 R ♭3 5

Cm7
C G E♭ B♭
R 5 ♭3 ♭7

Cm7
C B♭ G E♭
R ♭7 5 ♭3

Minor Seventh Chords with Alterations

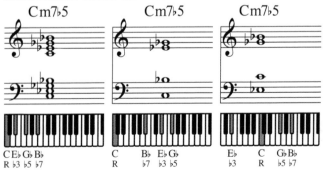

Cm7♭5
C E♭ G♭ B♭
R ♭3 ♭5 ♭7

Cm7♭5
C B♭ E♭ G♭
R ♭7 ♭3 ♭5

Cm7♭5
E♭ C G♭ B♭
♭3 R ♭5 ♭7

C

Minor-Major Seventh [m(maj7), m/M7] [R–♭3–5–7]

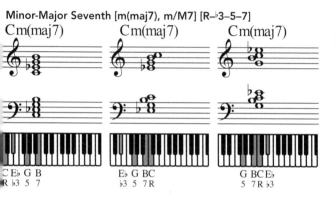

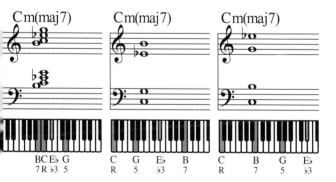

C

Diminished Seventh (°7) [R–♭3–♭5–♭♭7]

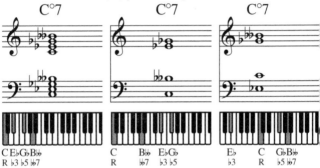

C°7	C°7	C°7

C E♭ G♭ B♭♭
R ♭3 ♭5 ♭♭7

C   B♭♭   E♭ G♭
R   ♭♭7   ♭3 ♭5

E♭   C   G♭ B♭♭
♭3   R   ♭5 ♭♭7

Ninth Chords

Dominant Ninth (9) [R–3–5–♭7–9]

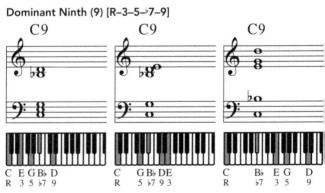

C9	C9	C9

C E G B♭ D
R 3 5 ♭7 9

C   G B♭ D E
R   5 ♭7 9 3

C   B♭   E G   D
R   ♭7   3 5   9

C

Dominant Ninth Chords with Alterations

C9♯5   C9♯5   C9♯5

Major Ninth (maj9, M9, ma9, 9) [R–3–5–7–9]

Cmaj9   Cmaj9   Cmaj9

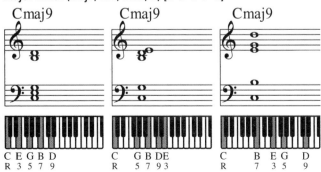

| C | E | G♯ | B♭ | D | | C | | G♯ | E | B♭ | D | | C | | B♭ | E | G♯ | | D |
| R | 3 | ♯5 | ♭7 | 9 | | R | | ♯5 | 3 | ♭7 | 9 | | R | | ♭7 | 3 | ♯5 | | 9 |

| C | E | G | B | D | | C | | G | B | DE | | C | | B | E | G | | D |
| R | 3 | 5 | 7 | 9 | | R | | 5 | 7 | 93 | | R | | 7 | 3 | 5 | | 9 |

C

Minor Ninth (m9, min9, -9) [R–♭3–5–♭7–9]

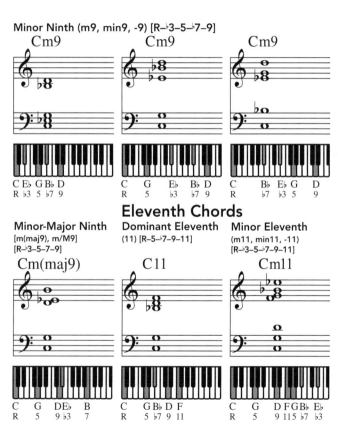

Cm9

Cm9

Cm9

C	E♭	G	B♭	D
R	♭3	5	♭7	9

C	G	E♭	B♭	D
R	5	♭3	♭7	9

C	B♭	E♭	G	D
R	♭7	♭3	5	9

Eleventh Chords

Minor-Major Ninth [m(maj9), m/M9] [R–♭3–5–7–9]

Dominant Eleventh (11) [R–5–♭7–9–11]

Minor Eleventh (m11, min11, -11) [R–♭3–5–♭7–9–11]

Cm(maj9)

C11

Cm11

C	G	D	E♭	B
R	5	9	♭3	7

C	G	B♭	D	F
R	5	♭7	9	11

C	G	D	F	G	B♭	B♭
R	5	9	11	5	♭7	♭3

C

Thirteenth Chords

Dominant Thirteenth (13) [R–3–5–♭7–9–13]

Major Thirteenth (maj13, M13, ma13) [R–3–5–7–9–13]

Minor Thirteenth (m13, min13, -13) [R–♭3–5–♭7–9–11–13]

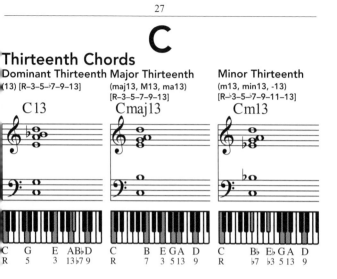

Sixth Chords

Sixth Chords (6) [R–3–5–6]

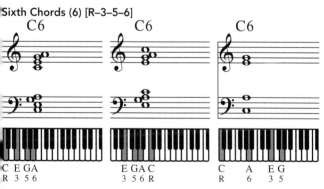

C

Six-Nine Chords ($^6_9$) [R–3–5–6–9]

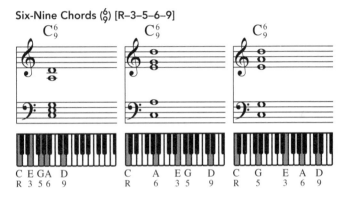

C^6_9 C^6_9 C^6_9

C E GA D
R 3 5 6 9

C A E G D
R 6 3 5 9

C G E A D
R 5 3 6 9

Minor Sixth Chords (m6) [R–♭3–5–6]

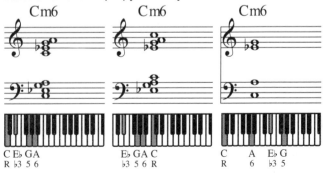

Cm6   Cm6   Cm6

C E♭ GA
R ♭3 5 6

E♭ GA C
♭3 5 6 R

C A E♭ G
R 6 ♭3 5

C

Minor Six-Nine Chords (m⁶₉) [R–♭3–5–6–9]

Power Chords ("5" Chords) [R–5]

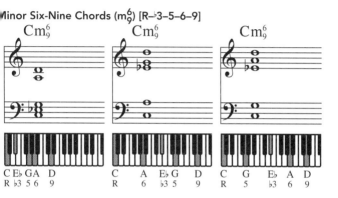

C

Suspended (sus) and add Chords

Sus2 [R–2–5]

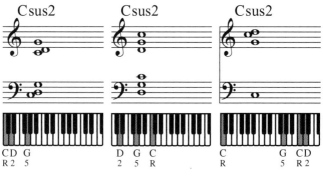

Sus4 [R–4–5]

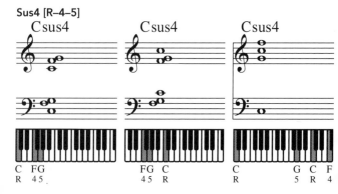

C

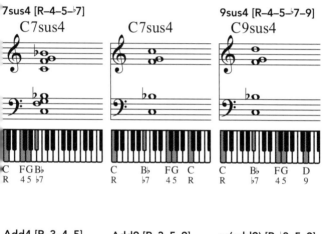

7sus4 [R–4–5–♭7]
C7sus4

C7sus4

9sus4 [R–4–5–♭7–9]
C9sus4

C	FG B♭
R	4 5 ♭7

C	B♭	FG	C
R	♭7	4 5	R

C	B♭	FG	D
R	♭7	4 5	9

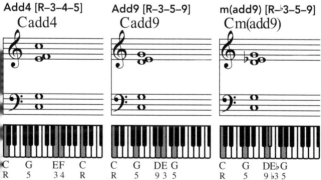

Add4 [R–3–4–5]
Cadd4

Add9 [R–3–5–9]
Cadd9

m(add9) [R–♭3–5–9]
Cm(add9)

C	G	EF	C
R	5	3 4	R

C	G	DE	G
R	5	9 3	5

C	G	DE♭	G
R	5	9 ♭3	5

C#/D♭

Triads

Major [R–3–5]

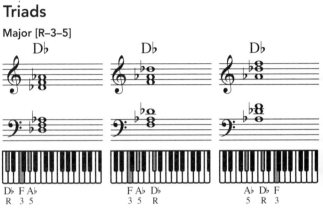

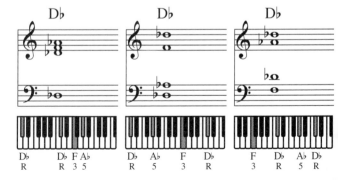

C#/D♭

Minor (m, -) [R–♭3–5]

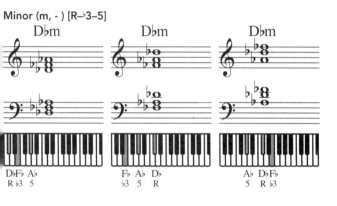

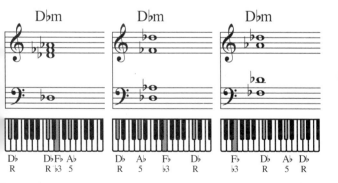

C#/D♭

Diminished (°, dim) [R–♭3–♭5]

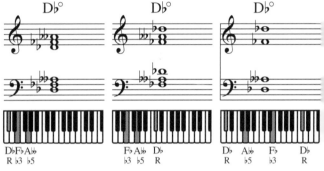

Augmented (+, aug) [R–3–#5]

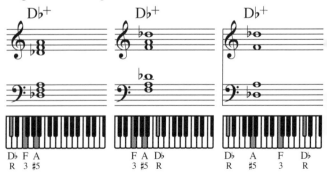

C#/Db

Seventh Chords

Dominant Seventh (7) [R–3–5–♭7]

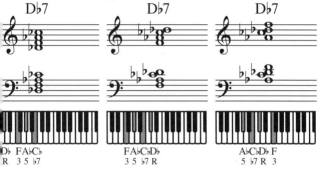

Db7   Db7   Db7

Db FAbCb
R 3 5 ♭7

FAbCbDb
3 5 ♭7 R

AbCbDb F
5 ♭7 R 3

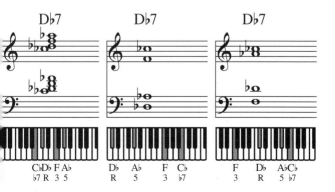

Db7   Db7   Db7

CbDb F Ab
♭7 R 3 5

Db   Ab   F   Cb
R   5   3   ♭7

F   Db   AbCb
3   R   5 ♭7

C#/Db

Dominant Seventh Chords with Alterations

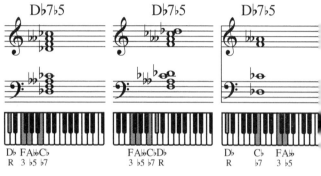

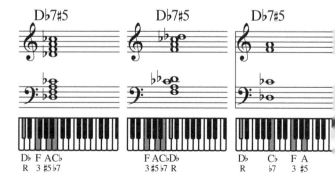

C#/Db

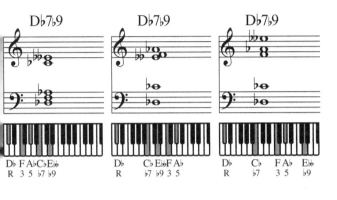

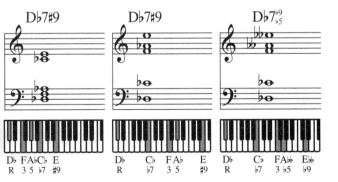

C#/Db

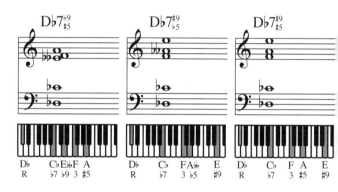

Db7b9#5

Db | Cb Eb | Bb F | A
R | b7 b9 | 3 | #5

Db7#9b5

Db | Cb | F A | Bb | E
R | b7 | 3 b5 | | #9

Db7#9#5

Db | Cb | F A | E
R | b7 | 3 #5 | #9

Major Seventh (maj7, M7, ma7, 7) [R–3–5–7]

Dbmaj7

Db | F | Ab | C
R | 3 | 5 | 7

Dbmaj7

F | Ab | C Db
3 | 5 | 7 R

Dbmaj7

Ab | C Db | F
5 | 7 R | 3

C#/Db

Dbmaj7   Dbmaj7   Dbmaj7

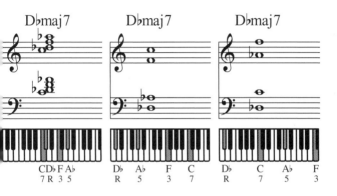

CDb F Ab
7 R 3 5

Db   Ab   F   C
R   5   3   7

Db   C   Ab   F
R   7   5   3

Major Seventh Chords with Alterations

Dbmaj7b5   Dbmaj7b5   Dbmaj7b5

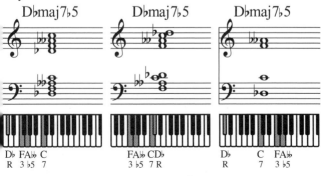

Db FAbb C
R 3 b5 7

FAbb CDb
3 b5 7 R

Db   C   FAbb
R   7   3 b5

C#/D♭

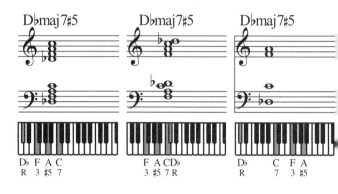

D♭maj7#5	D♭maj7#5	D♭maj7#5
D♭ F A C	F A C D♭	D♭ C F A
R 3 #5 7	3 #5 7 R	R 7 3 #5

Minor Seventh (m7, min7, -7) [R–♭3–5–♭7]

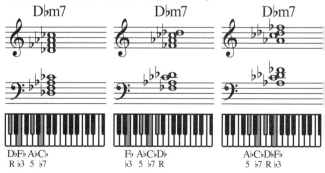

D♭m7	D♭m7	D♭m7
D♭ F♭ A♭ C♭	F♭ A♭ C♭ D♭	A♭ C♭ D♭ F♭
R ♭3 5 ♭7	♭3 5 ♭7 R	5 ♭7 R ♭3

C#/D♭

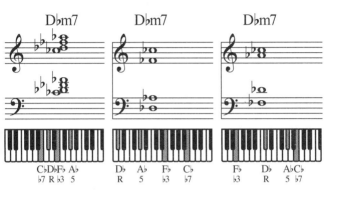

D♭m7   D♭m7   D♭m7

C♭D♭F♭ A♭
♭7 R ♭3   5

D♭   A♭   F♭   C♭
R   5   ♭3   ♭7

F♭   D♭   A♭C♭
♭3   R   5 ♭7

Minor Seventh Chords with Alterations

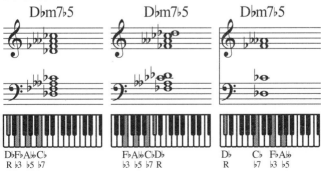

D♭m7♭5   D♭m7♭5   D♭m7♭5

D♭F♭A♭♭C♭
R ♭3 ♭5 ♭7

F♭A♭♭C♭D♭
♭3 ♭5 ♭7 R

D♭   C♭   F♭A♭♭
R   ♭7   ♭3 ♭5

C♯/D♭

Minor-Major Seventh [m(maj7), m/M7] [R–♭3–5–7]

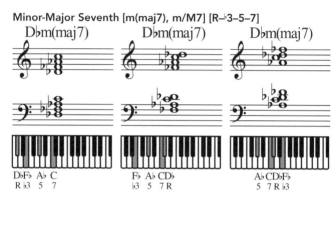

D♭m(maj7)

D♭m(maj7)

D♭m(maj7)

D♭ F♭ A♭ C
R ♭3 5 7

F♭ A♭ C D♭
♭3 5 7 R

A♭ C D♭ F♭
5 7 R ♭3

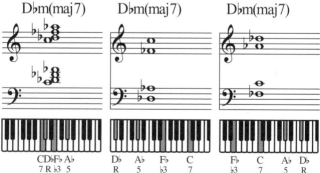

D♭m(maj7)

D♭m(maj7)

D♭m(maj7)

C D♭ F♭ A♭
7 R ♭3 5

D♭   A♭   F♭   C
R   5   ♭3   7

F♭   C   A♭   D♭
♭3   7   5   R

C#/Db

Diminished Seventh (°7) [R–♭3–♭5–♭♭7]

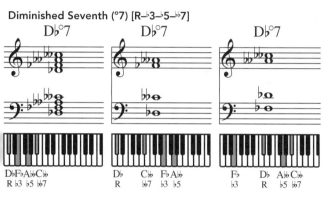

Ninth Chords

Dominant Ninth (9) [R–3–5–♭7–9]

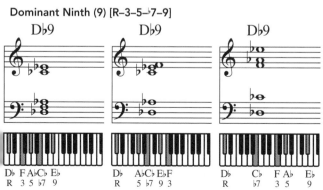

C#/Db

Dominant Ninth Chords with Alterations

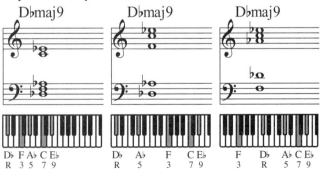

Db9#5   Db9#5   Db9#5

Db F A Cb Eb
R 3 #5 b7 9

Db Cb F A Eb
R   b7 3 #5 9

F Cb Eb A Db
3 b7   9 #5 R

Major Ninth (maj9, M9, ma9, 9) [R–3–5–7–9]

Dbmaj9   Dbmaj9   Dbmaj9

Db F Ab C Eb
R   3 5 7 9

Db Ab F C Eb
R   5   3 7 9

F Db Ab C Eb
3 R   5 7 9

C#/Db

Minor Ninth (m9, min9, -9) [R–b3–5–b7–9]

Dbm9

Dbm9

Dbm9

Db Fb Ab Cb Eb
R b3 5 b7   9

Db Cb Fb Ab Eb
R   b7 b3 5   9

Fb   Db Ab Cb Eb
b3   R   5 b7 9

Eleventh Chords

Minor-Major Ninth
[m(maj9), m/M9]
[R–b3–5–7–9]

Dbm(maj9)

Db Ab Eb Fb   C
R   5   9 b3   7

Dominant Eleventh
(11) [R–5–b7–9–11]

Db11

Db Ab Cb Eb Gb
R   5 b7 9 11

Minor Eleventh
(m11, min11, -11)
[R–b3–5–b7–9–11]

Dbm11

Db Ab Eb Gb Ab Cb Fb
R   5   9 11 5 b7 b3

C#/Db

Thirteenth Chords

Dominant Thirteenth
(13) [R–3–5–♭7–9–13]

Major Thirteenth
(maj13, M13, ma13)
[R–3–5–7–9–13]

Minor Thirteenth
(m13, min13, -13)
[R–♭3–5–♭7–9–11–13]

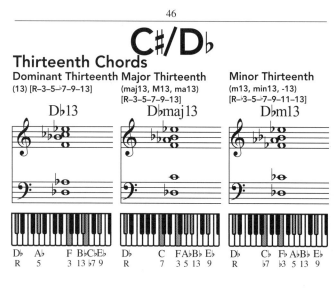

Sixth Chords

Sixth Chords (6) [R–3–5–6]

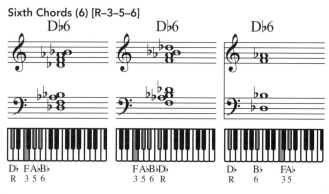

C#/Db

Six-Nine Chords (⁶₉) [R–3–5–6–9]

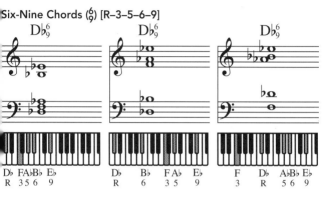

Db⁶₉   Db⁶₉   Db⁶₉

Db FAbBb Eb
R 3 5 6   9

Db   Bb   FAb   Eb
R   6   3 5   9

F   Db   AbBb Eb
3   R   5 6 9

Minor Sixth Chords (m6) [R–b3–5–6]

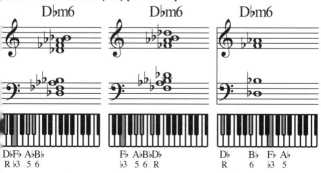

Dbm6   Dbm6   Dbm6

DbFb AbBb
R b3 5 6

Fb AbBbDb
b3 5 6 R

Db   Bb   Fb Ab
R   6   b3 5

C♯/D♭

Minor Six-Nine Chords (m$_9^6$) [R–♭3–5–6–9]

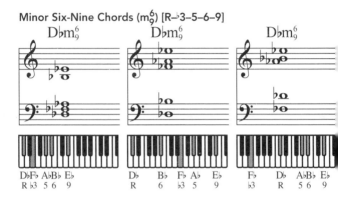

Power Chords ("5" Chords) [R–5]

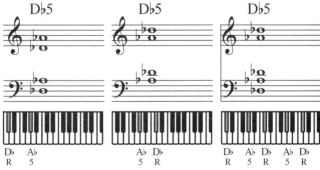

C♯/D♭

Suspended (sus) and add Chords

Sus2 [R–2–5]

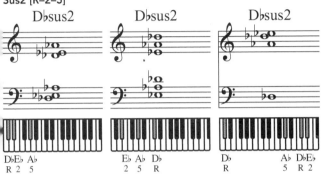

D♭sus2   D♭sus2   D♭sus2

D♭E♭ A♭   E♭ A♭ D♭   D♭   A♭ D♭E♭
R 2 5   2 5 R   R   5 R 2

Sus4 [R–4–5]

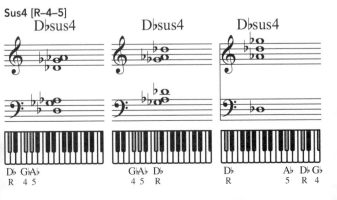

D♭sus4   D♭sus4   D♭sus4

D♭ G♭A♭   G♭A♭ D♭   D♭   A♭ D♭ G♭
R 4 5   4 5 R   R   5 R 4

C#/Db

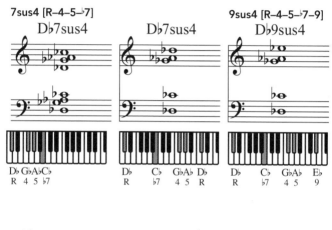

7sus4 [R–4–5–♭7]
Db7sus4   Db7sus4

Db GbAbCb
R   4   5   ♭7

Db   Cb   GbAb   Db
R   ♭7   4   5   R

9sus4 [R–4–5–♭7–9]
Db9sus4

Db   Cb   GbAb   Eb
R   ♭7   4   5   9

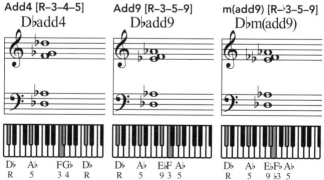

Add4 [R–3–4–5]
Dbadd4

Db   Ab   FGb   Db
R   5   3 4   R

Add9 [R–3–5–9]
Dbadd9

Db   Ab   EbF   Ab
R   5   9 3   5

m(add9) [R–♭3–5–9]
Dbm(add9)

Db   Ab   EbFb   Ab
R   5   9 ♭3   5

D

Triads

Major [R–3–5]

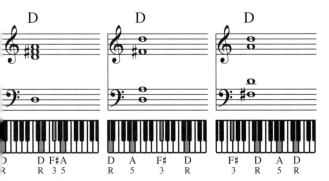

D

Minor (m, -) [R–♭3–5]

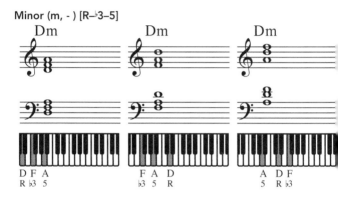

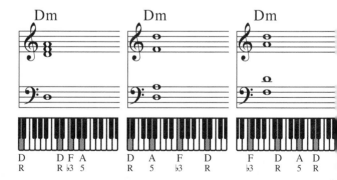

D

Diminished (°, dim) [R–♭3–♭5]

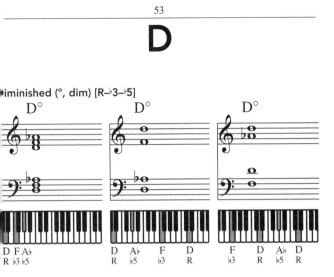

D°
D°
D°

D F A♭
R ♭3 ♭5

D A♭ F D
R ♭5 ♭3 R

F D A♭ D
♭3 R ♭5 R

Augmented (+, aug) [R–3–♯5]

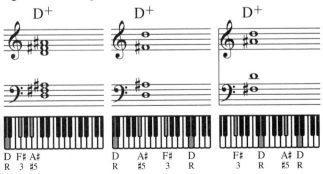

D+
D+
D+

D F♯ A♯
R 3 ♯5

D A♯ F♯ D
R ♯5 3 R

F♯ D A♯ D
3 R ♯5 R

D

Seventh Chords

Dominant Seventh (7) [R–3–5–♭7]

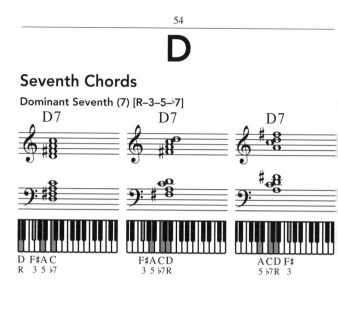

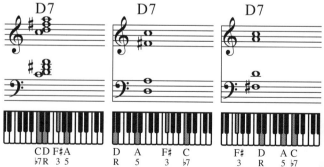

D

Dominant Seventh Chords with Alterations

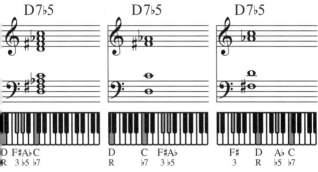

D7♭5	D7♭5	D7♭5
D F#A♭C	D C F#A♭	F# D A♭ C
R 3 ♭5 ♭7	R ♭7 3 ♭5	3 R ♭5 ♭7

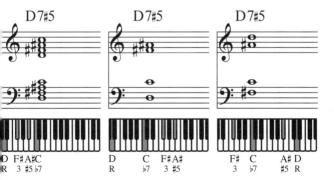

D7#5	D7#5	D7#5
D F#A#C	D C F#A#	F# C A# D
R 3 #5 ♭7	R ♭7 3 #5	3 ♭7 #5 R

D

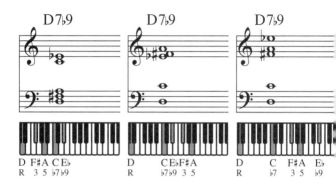

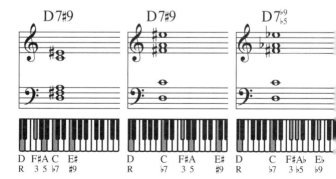

D

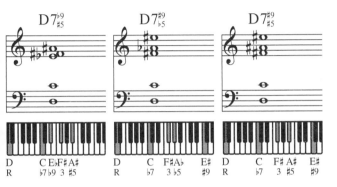

$D7^{\flat9}_{\sharp5}$ $D7^{\sharp9}_{\flat5}$ $D7^{\sharp9}_{\sharp5}$

D   C E♭ F♯ A♯
R   ♭7 ♭9 3 #5

D   C F♯ A♭   E♯
R   ♭7 3 ♭5   #9

D   C F♯ A♯   E♯
R   ♭7 3 #5   #9

Major Seventh (maj7, M7, ma7, 7) [R–3–5–7]

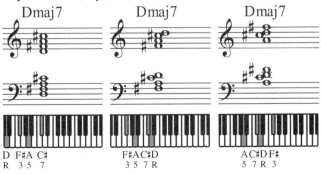

Dmaj7   Dmaj7   Dmaj7

D F♯A C♯
R 3 5 7

F♯A C♯D
3 5 7 R

A C♯D F♯
5 7 R 3

D

Dmaj7

Dmaj7

Dmaj7

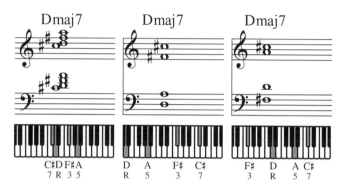

C#D F#A	D	A	F#	C#	F#	D	A	C#
7 R 3 5	R	5	3	7	3	R	5	7

Major Seventh Chords with Alterations

Dmaj7♭5

Dmaj7♭5

Dmaj7♭5

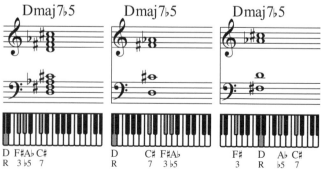

D F#A♭ C#	D	C# F#A♭	F#	D	A♭ C#
R 3♭5 7	R	7 3♭5	3	R	♭5 7

D

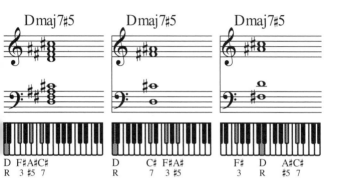

Dmaj7♯5   Dmaj7♯5   Dmaj7♯5

D F♯A♯C♯   D   C♯ F♯A♯   F♯   D   A♯C♯
R 3 ♯5 7   R   7   3 ♯5   3   R   ♯5 7

Minor Seventh (m7, min7, -7) [R–♭3–5–♭7]

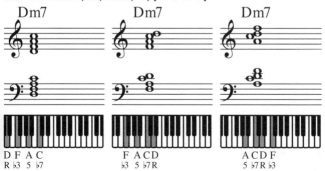

Dm7   Dm7   Dm7

D F A C   F A C D   A C D F
R ♭3 5 ♭7   ♭3 5 ♭7 R   5 ♭7 R ♭3

D

Dm7

Dm7

Dm7

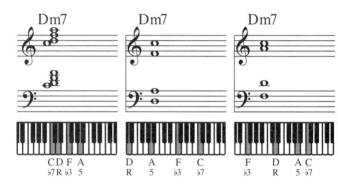

CD F A
♭7 R ♭3 5

D   A   F   C
R   5   ♭3   ♭7

F   D   A C
♭3   R   5 ♭7

Minor Seventh Chords with Alterations

Dm7♭5

Dm7♭5

Dm7♭5

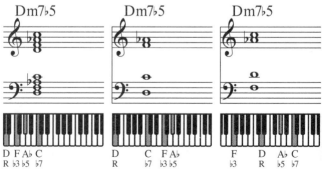

D F A♭ C
R ♭3 ♭5 ♭7

D   C   F A♭
R   ♭7   ♭3 ♭5

F   D   A♭ C
♭3   R   ♭5 ♭7

D

Minor-Major Seventh [m(maj7), m/M7] [R–♭3–5–7]

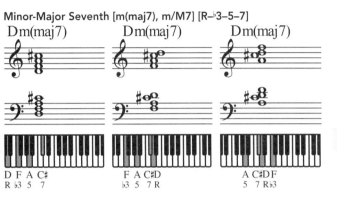

Dm(maj7)
D F A C♯
R ♭3 5 7

Dm(maj7)
F A C♯D
♭3 5 7 R

Dm(maj7)
A C♯DF
5 7 R♭3

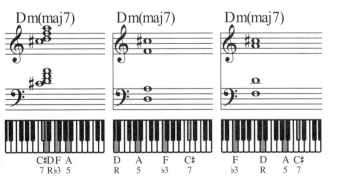

Dm(maj7)
C♯DF A
7 R♭3 5

Dm(maj7)
D A F C♯
R 5 ♭3 7

Dm(maj7)
F D A C♯
♭3 R 5 7

D

Diminished Seventh (°7) [R–♭3–♭5–♭♭7]

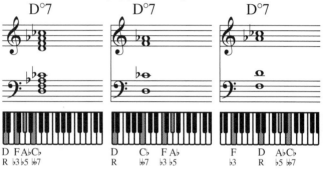

Ninth Chords

Dominant Ninth (9) [R–3–5–♭7–9]

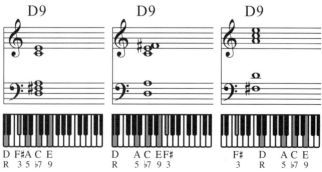

D

Dominant Ninth Chords with Alterations

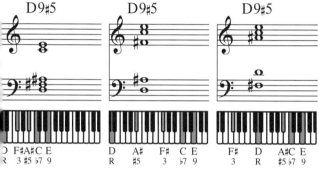

D9#5

D9#5

D9#5

Major Ninth (maj9, M9, ma9, 9) [R–3–5–7–9]

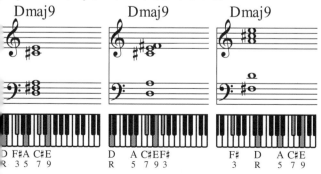

Dmaj9

Dmaj9

Dmaj9

D

Minor Ninth (m9, min9, -9) [R–♭3–5–♭7–9]

Dm9

Dm9

Dm9

Eleventh Chords

Minor-Major Ninth
[m(maj9), m/M9]
[R–♭3–5–7–9]

Dm(maj9)

Dominant Eleventh
(11) [R–5–♭7–9–11]

D11

Minor Eleventh
(m11, min11, -11)
[R–♭3–5–♭7–9–11]

Dm11

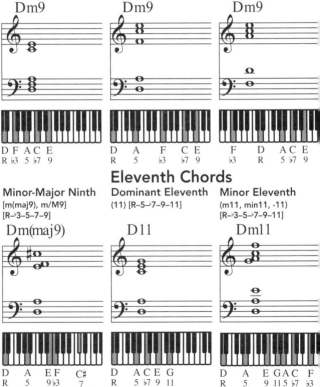

D

Thirteenth Chords

Dominant Thirteenth
(13) [R–3–5–♭7–9–13]

Major Thirteenth
(maj13, M13, ma13)
[R–3–5–7–9–13]

Minor Thirteenth
(m13, min13, -13)
[R–♭3–5–♭7–9–11–13]

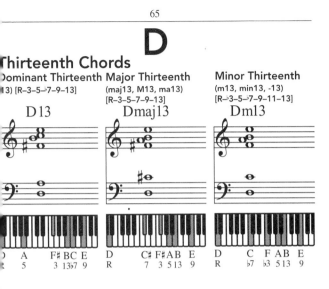

D13	Dmaj13	Dml3
D A F# BC E	D C# F#AB E	D C F AB E
R 5 3 13♭7 9	R 7 3 513 9	R ♭7 ♭3 513 9

Sixth Chords

Sixth Chords (6) [R–3–5–6]

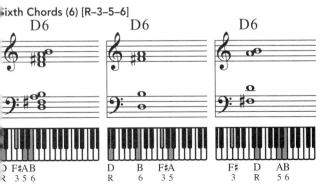

D6	D6	D6
D F#AB	D B F#A	F# D AB
R 3 5 6	R 6 3 5	3 R 5 6

D

Six-Nine Chords ($\frac{6}{9}$) [R–3–5–6–9]

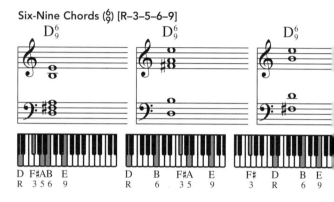

| D$_9^6$ | D$_9^6$ | D$_9^6$ |

| D | F# | A | B | | E | | D | | B | | F# | A | | E | | F# | | D | | B | | E |
| R | 3 | 5 | 6 | | 9 | | R | | 6 | | 3 | 5 | | 9 | | 3 | | R | | 6 | | 9 |

Minor Sixth Chords (m6) [R–♭3–5–6]

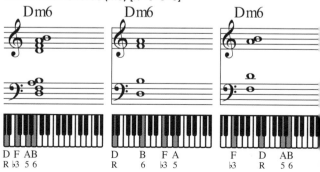

| Dm6 | Dm6 | Dm6 |

| D | F | | A | B | | D | | B | | F | A | | F | | D | | A | B |
| R | ♭3 | | 5 | 6 | | R | | 6 | | ♭3 | 5 | | ♭3 | | R | | 5 | 6 |

D

Minor Six-Nine Chords (m⁶₉) [R–♭3–5–6–9]

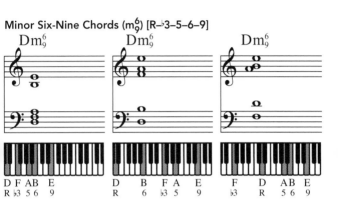

Dm_9^6 Dm_9^6 Dm_9^6

D F AB	E		D	B	F A	E		F	D	AB	E
R ♭3 5 6	9		R	6	♭3 5	9		♭3	R	5 6	9

Power Chords ("5" Chords) [R–5]

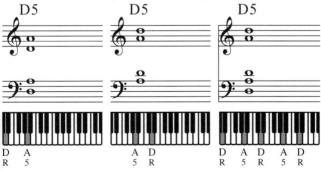

D5   D5   D5

D	A		A	D		D	A	D	A	D
R	5		5	R		R	5	R	5	R

D

Suspended (sus) and add Chords

Sus2 [R–2–5]

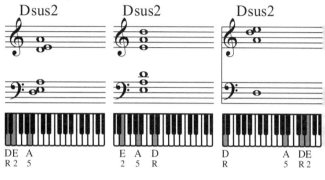

Sus4 [R–4–5]

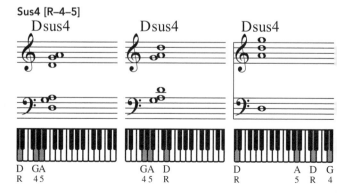

D

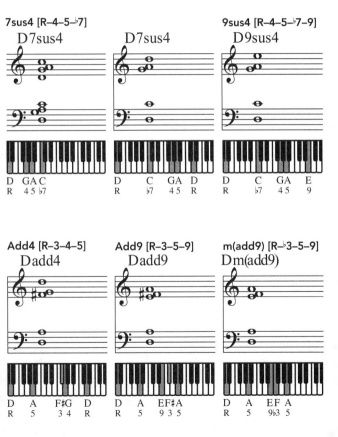

7sus4 [R–4–5–♭7]

D7sus4

D GAC
R 4 5 ♭7

D7sus4

D C GA D
R ♭7 4 5 R

9sus4 [R–4–5–♭7–9]

D9sus4

D C GA E
R ♭7 4 5 9

Add4 [R–3–4–5]

Dadd4

D A F#G D
R 5 3 4 R

Add9 [R–3–5–9]

Dadd9

D A EF#A
R 5 9 3 5

m(add9) [R–♭3–5–9]

Dm(add9)

D A EF A
R 5 9♭3 5

Triads

Major [R–3–5]

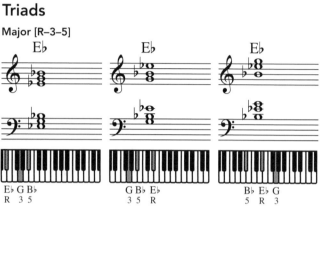

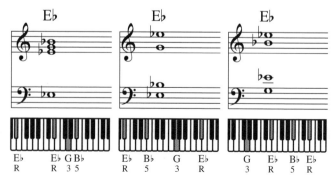

D♯/E♭

Minor (m, -) [R–♭3–5]

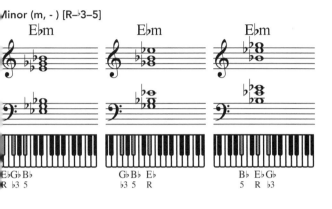

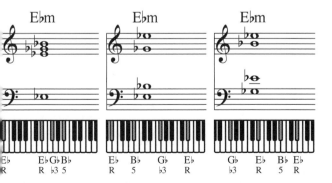

D#/E♭

Diminished (°, dim) [R–♭3–♭5]

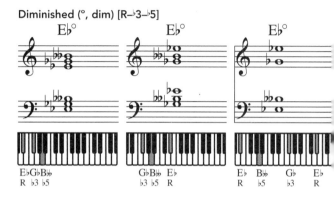

E♭G♭B♭♭
R ♭3 ♭5

G♭B♭♭ E♭
♭3 ♭5 R

E♭ B♭♭ G♭ E♭
R ♭5 ♭3 R

Augmented (+, aug) [R–3–#5]

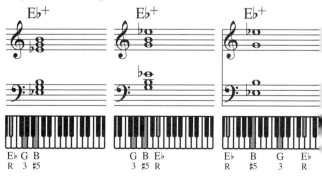

E♭ G B
R 3 #5

G B E♭
3 #5 R

E♭ B G E♭
R #5 3 R

D#/E♭

Seventh Chords

Dominant Seventh (7) [R–3–5–♭7]

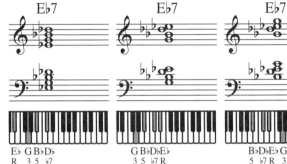

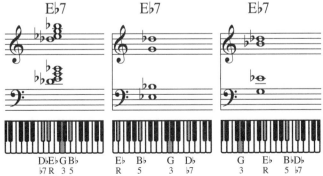

D♯/E♭

Dominant Seventh Chords with Alterations

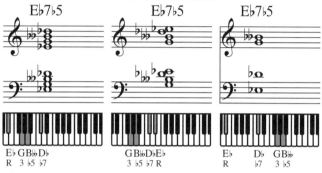

Eb7b5   Eb7b5   Eb7b5

Eb GBbb Db
R 3 b5 b7

GBbbDbEb
3 b5 b7 R

Eb   Db   GBbb
R   b7   3 b5

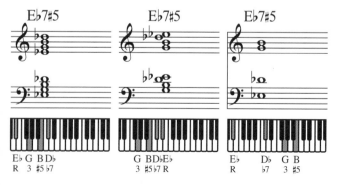

Eb7#5   Eb7#5   Eb7#5

Eb G B Db
R 3 #5 b7

G BDbEb
3 #5b7 R

Eb   Db   G B
R   b7   3 #5

D#/Eb

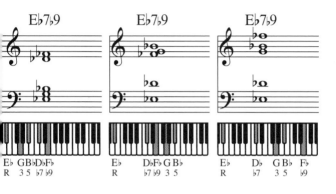

Eb7b9   Eb7b9   Eb7b9

Eb GBbDbFb   Eb   DbFb GBb   Eb   Db   GBb   Fb
R   3 5 b7 b9   R   b7 b9 3 5   R   b7   3 5   b9

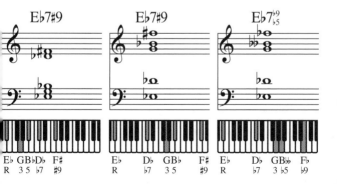

Eb7#9   Eb7#9   Eb7b9b5

Eb GBbDb F#   Eb   Db   GBb   F#   Eb   Db   GBb   Fb
R   3 5 b7 #9   R   b7   3 5   #9   R   b7   3 b5   b9

D♯/E♭

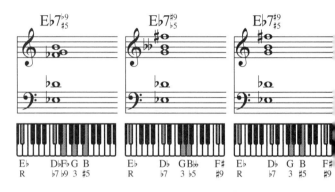

E♭7♭9♯5   E♭7♯9♭5   E♭7♯9♯5

| E♭ | D♭ F♭ G B | E♭ | D♭ G B♭♭ | F♯ | E♭ | D♭ G B | F♯ |
| R | ♭7 ♭9 3 ♯5 | R | ♭7 3 ♭5 | ♯9 | R | ♭7 3 ♯5 | ♯9 |

Major Seventh (maj7, M7, ma7, 7) [R–3–5–7]

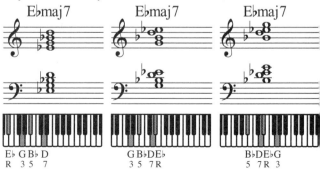

E♭maj7   E♭maj7   E♭maj7

| E♭ G B♭ D | G B♭ D E♭ | B♭ D E♭ G |
| R 3 5 7 | 3 5 7 R | 5 7 R 3 |

D#/Eb

Ebmaj7

Ebmaj7

Ebmaj7

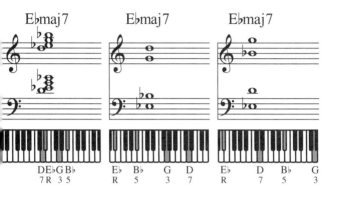

DEbGBb
7R 3 5

Eb Bb G D
R   5   3 7

Eb D Bb G
R   7 5   3

Major Seventh Chords with Alterations

Ebmaj7b5

Ebmaj7b5

Ebmaj7b5

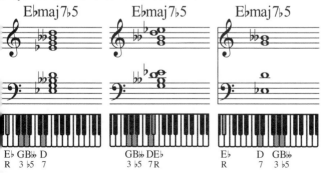

Eb GBbb D
R 3 b5 7

GBbb DEb
3 b5 7R

Eb D GBbb
R   7 3 b5

D♯/E♭

Ebmaj7#5   Ebmaj7#5   Ebmaj7#5

Minor Seventh (m7, min7, -7) [R–♭3–5–♭7]

Ebm7   Ebm7   Ebm7

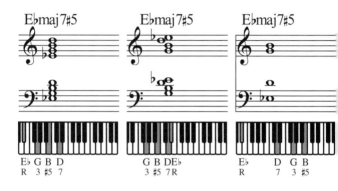

Eb G B D   G B DEb   Eb   D G B
R 3 #5 7   3 #5 7R   R   7 3 #5

Eb Gb Bb Db   Gb Bb Db Eb   Bb Db Eb Gb
R b3 5 b7   b3 5 b7 R   5 b7 R b3

D♯/E♭

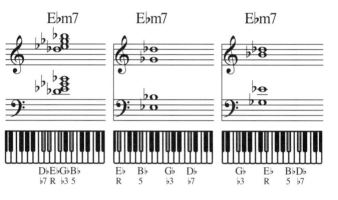

E♭m7	E♭m7	E♭m7

D♭E♭G♭B♭
♭7 R ♭3 5

E♭ B♭ G♭ D♭
R 5 ♭3 ♭7

G♭ E♭ B♭D♭
♭3 R 5 ♭7

Minor Seventh Chords with Alterations

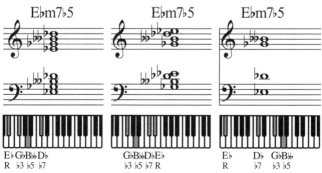

E♭m7♭5	E♭m7♭5	E♭m7♭5

E♭ G♭B♭♭D♭
R ♭3 ♭5 ♭7

G♭B♭♭D♭E♭
♭3 ♭5 ♭7 R

E♭ D♭ G♭B♭♭
R ♭7 ♭3 ♭5

D#/E♭

Minor-Major Seventh [m(maj7), m/M7] [R–♭3–5–7]

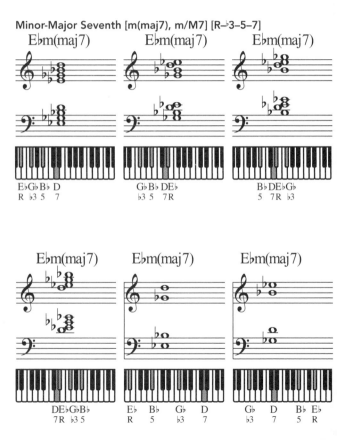

E♭m(maj7)

E♭m(maj7)

E♭m(maj7)

E♭ G♭ B♭ D
R ♭3 5 7

G♭ B♭ D E♭
♭3 5 7 R

B♭ D E♭ G♭
5 7 R ♭3

E♭m(maj7)

E♭m(maj7)

E♭m(maj7)

D E♭ G♭ B♭
7 R ♭3 5

E♭   B♭   G♭   D
R   5   ♭3   7

G♭   D   B♭   E♭
♭3   7   5   R

D♯/E♭

Diminished Seventh (°7) [R–♭3–♭5–♭♭7]

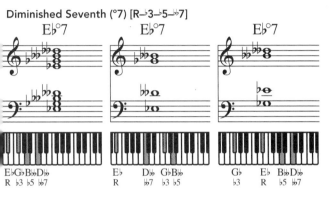

E♭°7 E♭°7 E♭°7

E♭ G♭ B♭♭ D♭♭
R ♭3 ♭5 ♭♭7

E♭ D♭♭ G♭ B♭♭
R ♭♭7 ♭3 ♭5

G♭ E♭ B♭♭ D♭♭
♭3 R ♭5 ♭♭7

Ninth Chords

Dominant Ninth (9) [R–3–5–♭7–9]

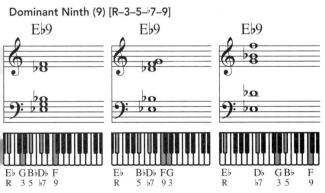

E♭9 E♭9 E♭9

E♭ G B♭ D♭ F
R 3 5 ♭7 9

E♭ B♭ D♭ F G
R 5 ♭7 9 3

E♭ D♭ G B♭ F
R ♭7 3 5 9

D♯/E♭

Dominant Ninth Chords with Alterations

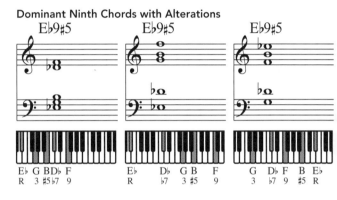

E♭9♯5

E♭9♯5

E♭9♯5

E♭ G B D♭ F	E♭ D♭ G B F	G D♭ F B E♭
R 3 ♯5 ♭7 9	R ♭7 3 ♯5 9	3 ♭7 9 ♯5 R

Major Ninth (maj9, M9, ma9, 9) [R–3–5–7–9]

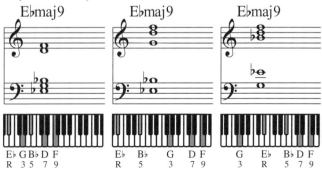

E♭maj9

E♭maj9

E♭maj9

E♭ G B♭ D F	E♭ B♭ G D F	G E♭ B♭ D F
R 3 5 7 9	R 5 3 7 9	3 R 5 7 9

D#/E♭

Minor Ninth (m9, min9, -9) [R–♭3–5–♭7–9]

E♭m9

E♭m9

E♭m9

E♭G♭B♭D♭ F
R ♭3 5 ♭7 9

E♭   D♭ G♭B♭   F
R   ♭7 ♭3 5   9

G♭   E♭   B♭D♭ F
♭3   R   5 ♭7 9

Eleventh Chords

Minor-Major Ninth [m(maj9), m/M9] [R–♭3–5–7–9]

Dominant Eleventh (11) [R–5–♭7–9–11]

Minor Eleventh (m11, min11, -11) [R–♭3–5–♭7–9–11]

E♭m(maj9)

E♭11

E♭m11

E♭   B♭   F G♭   D
R   5   9♭3   7

E♭   B♭D♭ F A♭
R   5 ♭7 9 11

E♭   B♭   F A♭B♭D♭ G♭
R   5   9 11 5 ♭7 ♭3

D♯/E♭

Thirteenth Chords

Dominant Thirteenth
(13) [R–3–5–♭7–9–13]

Major Thirteenth
(maj13, M13, ma13)
[R–3–5–7–9–13]

Minor Thirteenth
(m13, min13, -13)
[R–♭3–5–♭7–9–11–13]

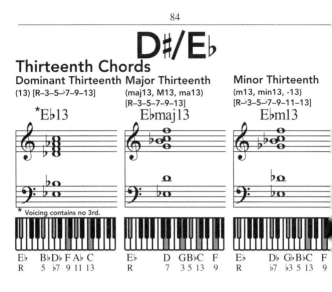

*E♭13

* Voicing contains no 3rd.

E♭ B♭D♭ F A♭ C
R   5 ♭7 9 11 13

E♭maj13

E♭   D GB♭C F
R   7 3 5 13 9

E♭m13

E♭   D♭ G♭B♭C F
R   ♭7 ♭3 5 13 9

Sixth Chords

Sixth Chords (6) [R–3–5–6]

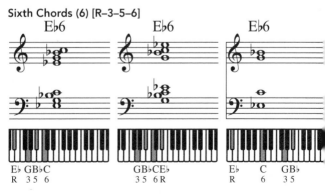

E♭6

E♭ GB♭C
R 3 5 6

E♭6

GB♭CE♭
3 5 6R

E♭6

E♭   C   GB♭
R   6   3 5

D♯/E♭

Six-Nine Chords ($^6_9$) [R–3–5–6–9]

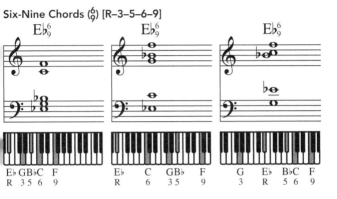

$E\flat^6_9$ $E\flat^6_9$ $E\flat^6_9$

E♭	G B♭ C	F
R	3 5 6	9

E♭	C	G B♭	F
R	6	3 5	9

G	E♭	B♭ C	F
3	R	5 6	9

Minor Sixth Chords (m6) [R–♭3–5–6]

E♭m6   E♭m6   E♭m6

E♭ G♭ B♭ C			
R ♭3 5 6			

G♭ B♭ C E♭
♭3 5 6 R

E♭	C	G♭ B♭
R	6	♭3 5

D♯/E♭

Minor Six-Nine Chords (m$_9^6$) [R–♭3–5–6–9]

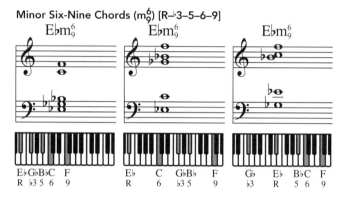

E♭m$_9^6$ E♭m$_9^6$ E♭m$_9^6$

E♭ G♭ B♭ C   F
R   ♭3 5 6   9

E♭   C   G♭ B♭   F
R   6   ♭3 5   9

G♭   E♭   B♭ C   F
♭3   R   5 6   9

Power Chords ("5" Chords) [R–5]

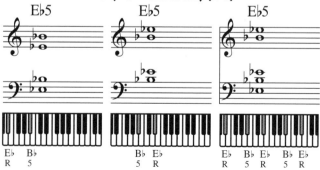

E♭5   E♭5   E♭5

E♭   B♭
R   5

B♭   E♭
5   R

E♭   B♭ E♭   B♭ E♭
R   5 R   5 R

D♯/E♭

Suspended (sus) and add Chords

Sus2 [R–2–5]

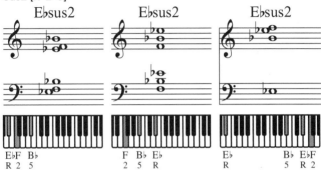

Sus4 [R–4–5]

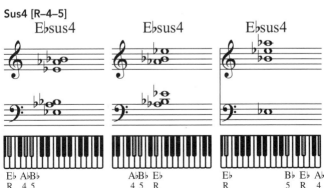

D♯/E♭

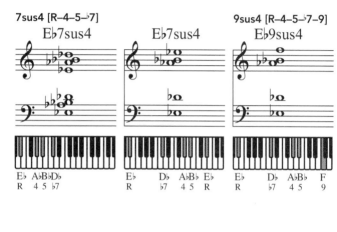

7sus4 [R–4–5–♭7]

E♭7sus4

E♭7sus4

E♭ A♭B♭D♭
R 4 5 ♭7

E♭ D♭ A♭B♭ E♭
R ♭7 4 5 R

9sus4 [R–4–5–♭7–9]

E♭9sus4

E♭ D♭ A♭B♭ F
R ♭7 4 5 9

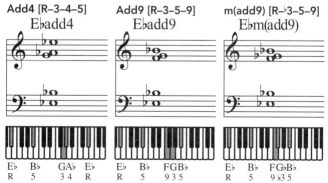

Add4 [R–3–4–5]

E♭add4

E♭ B♭ GA♭ E♭
R 5 3 4 R

Add9 [R–3–5–9]

E♭add9

E♭ B♭ FGB♭
R 5 935

m(add9) [R–♭3–5–9]

E♭m(add9)

E♭ B♭ FG♭B♭
R 5 9♭35

E

Triads

Major [R–3–5]

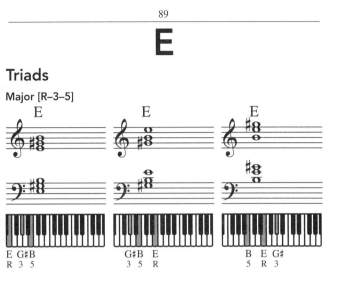

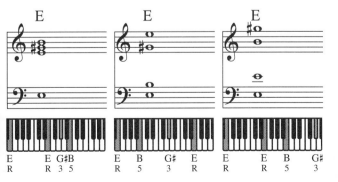

E

Minor (m, -) [R–♭3–5]

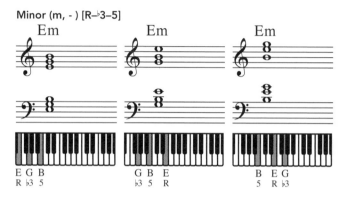

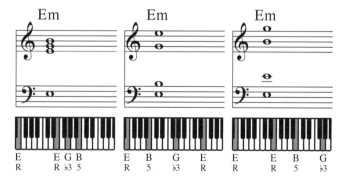

E

Diminished (°, dim) [R–♭3–♭5]

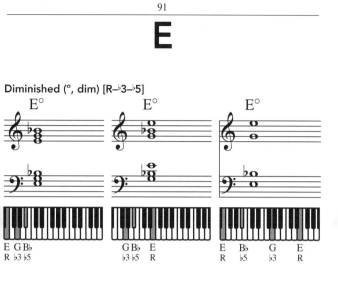

E°	E°	E°
E G B♭	G B♭ E	E B♭ G E
R ♭3 ♭5	♭3 ♭5 R	R ♭5 ♭3 R

Augmented (+, aug) [R–3–♯5]

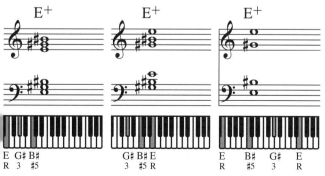

E+	E+	E+
E G♯ B♯	G♯ B♯ E	E B♯ G♯ E
R 3 ♯5	3 ♯5 R	R ♯5 3 R

E

Seventh Chords

Dominant Seventh (7) [R–3–5–♭7]

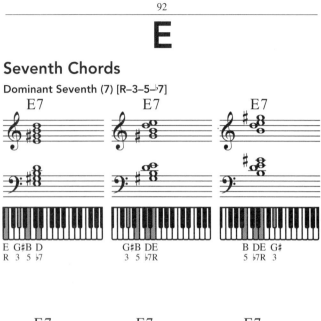

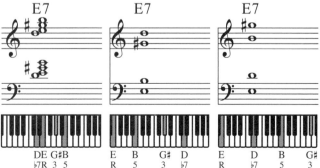

E

Dominant Seventh Chords with Alterations

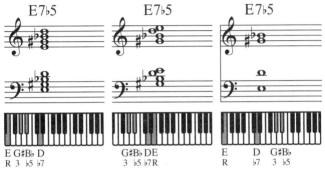

E7♭5

E7♭5

E7♭5

E G♯B♭ D
R 3 ♭5 ♭7

G♯B♭ DE
3 ♭5 ♭7R

E   D G♯B♭
R   ♭7 3 ♭5

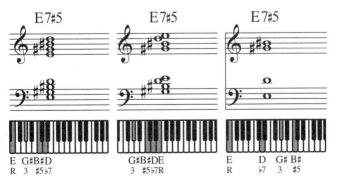

E7♯5

E7♯5

E7♯5

E G♯B♯D
R 3 ♯5♭7

G♯B♯DE
3 ♯5♭7R

E   D G♯ B♯
R   ♭7 3 ♯5

E

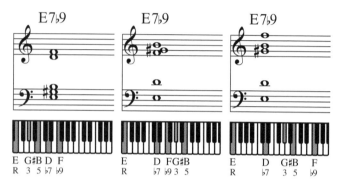

E7♭9 | E7♭9 | E7♭9

E | G#B D | F
R | 3 5 ♭7 | ♭9

E | D | FG#B
R | ♭7 | ♭9 3 5

E | D | G#B | F
R | ♭7 | 3 5 | ♭9

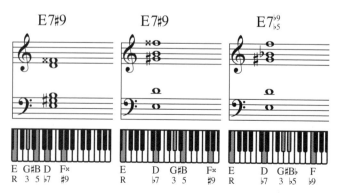

E7#9 | E7#9 | E7♭9♭5

E | G#B D | F×
R | 3 5 ♭7 | #9

E | D | G#B | F×
R | ♭7 | 3 5 | #9

E | D | G#B♭ | F
R | ♭7 | 3 ♭5 | ♭9

E

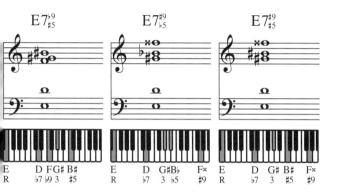

$E7^{\flat 9}_{\sharp 5}$ — E7♯5♭9 — R ♭7 ♭9 3 ♯5 (E D F G♯ B♯)

$E7^{\sharp 9}_{\flat 5}$ — R ♭7 3 ♭5 ♯9 (E D G♯ B♭ F×)

$E7^{\sharp 9}_{\sharp 5}$ — R ♭7 3 ♯5 ♯9 (E D G♯ B♯ F×)

Major Seventh (maj7, M7, ma7, 7) [R–3–5–7]

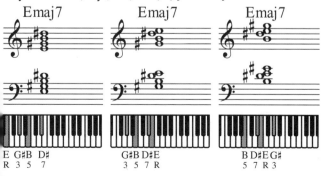

Emaj7 — E G♯B D♯ — R 3 5 7

Emaj7 — G♯B D♯E — 3 5 7 R

Emaj7 — B D♯E G♯ — 5 7 R 3

E

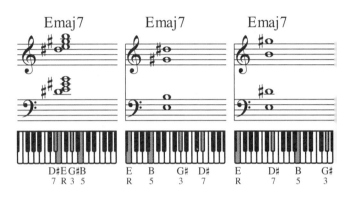

Emaj7	Emaj7	Emaj7
D#E G#B	E B G# D#	E D# B G#
7 R 3 5	R 5 3 7	R 7 5 3

Major Seventh Chords with Alterations

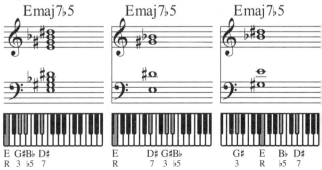

Emaj7♭5	Emaj7♭5	Emaj7♭5
E G#B♭ D#	E D# G#B♭	G# E B♭ D#
R 3 ♭5 7	R 7 3 ♭5	3 R ♭5 7

E

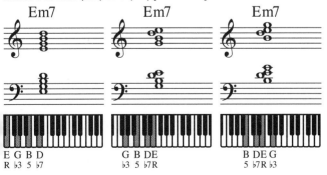

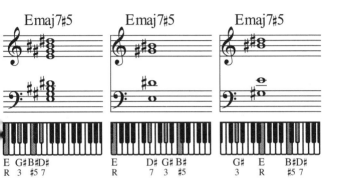

Emaj7#5   Emaj7#5   Emaj7#5

E G#B#D#   E   D# G# B#   G#   E   B#D#
R 3 #5 7   R   7   3   #5   3   R   #5 7

Minor Seventh (m7, min7, -7) [R–♭3–5–♭7]

Em7   Em7   Em7

E G B D   G B DE   B DE G
R ♭3 5 ♭7   ♭3 5 ♭7R   5 ♭7R ♭3

E

Em7   Em7   Em7

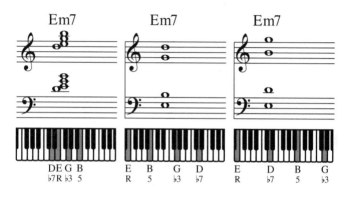

Minor Seventh Chords with Alterations

Em7♭5   Em7♭5   Em7♭5

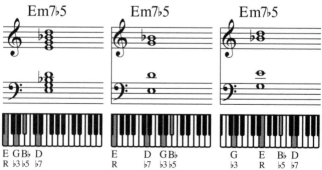

E

Minor-Major Seventh [m(maj7), m/M7] [R–♭3–5–7]

Em(maj7)

Em(maj7)

Em(maj7)

E G B D#
R ♭3 5 7

G B D#E
♭3 5 7 R

B D#EG
5 7 R♭3

Em(maj7)

Em(maj7)

Em(maj7)

D#EG B
7 R♭3 5

E B G D#
R 5 ♭3 7

E D# B G
R 7 5 ♭3

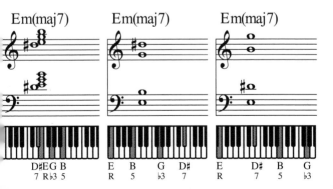

E

Diminished Seventh (°7) [R–♭3–♭5–♭♭7]

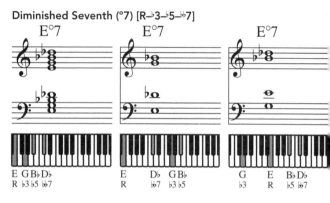

E°7   E°7   E°7

E G B♭ D♭
R ♭3 ♭5 ♭♭7

E   D♭ G B♭
R   ♭♭7 ♭3 ♭5

G   E   B♭ D♭
♭3   R   ♭5 ♭♭7

Ninth Chords

Dominant Ninth (9) [R–3–5–♭7–9]

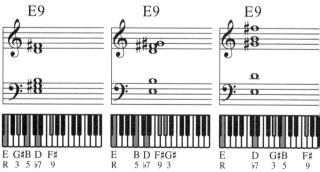

E9   E9   E9

E G♯ B D   F♯
R 3 5 ♭7   9

E   B D F♯ G♯
R   5 ♭7 9 3

E   D   G♯ B   F♯
R   ♭7   3 5   9

E

Dominant Ninth Chords with Alterations

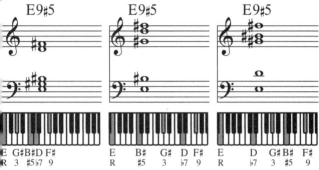

Major Ninth (maj9, M9, ma9, 9) [R–3–5–7–9]

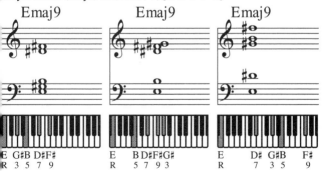

E

Minor Ninth (m9, min9, -9) [R–♭3–5–♭7–9]

Em9

Em9

Em9

E	G	B	D	F#
R	♭3	5	♭7	9

E	B	G	D	F#
R	5	♭3	♭7	9

E	D	G	B	F#
R	♭7	♭3	5	9

Eleventh Chords

Minor-Major Ninth
[m(maj9), m/M9]
[R–♭3–5–7–9]

Dominant Eleventh
(11) [R–5–♭7–9–11]

Minor Eleventh
(m11, min11, -11)
[R–♭3–5–♭7–9–11]

Em(maj9)

E11

Em11

E	B	F#G	D#
R	5	9 ♭3	7

E	B D F#A
R	5 ♭7 9 11

E	B	F#AB D	G
R	5	9 11 5 ♭7	♭3

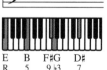

E

Thirteenth Chords

Dominant Thirteenth
(13) [R–3–5–♭7–9–13]

Major Thirteenth
(maj13, M13, ma13)
[R–3–5–7–9–13]

Minor Thirteenth
(m13, min13, -13)
[R–♭3–5–♭7–9–11–13]

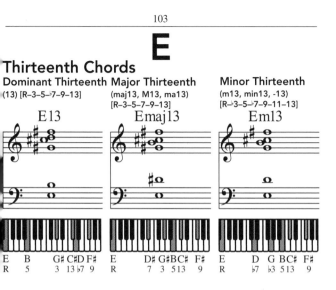

Sixth Chords

Sixth Chords (6) [R–3–5–6]

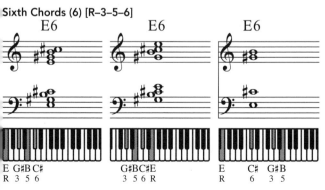

E

Six-Nine Chords ($^6_9$) [R–3–5–6–9]

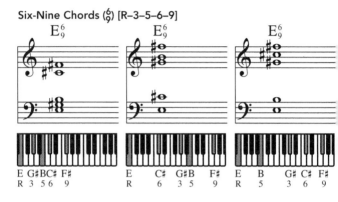

Minor Sixth Chords (m6) [R–♭3–5–6]

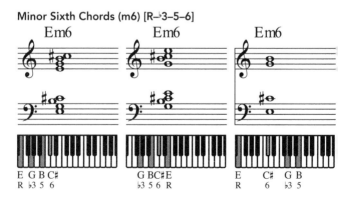

E

Minor Six-Nine Chords (m$_9^6$) [R–♭3–5–6–9]

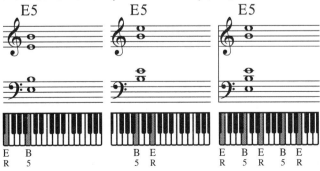

E

Suspended (sus) and add Chords

Sus2 [R–2–5]

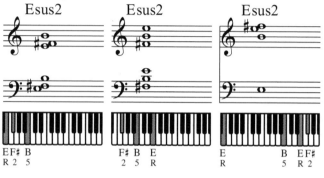

Esus2

E F# B
R 2 5

Esus2

F# B E
2 5 R

Esus2

E B E F#
R 5 R 2

Sus4 [R–4–5]

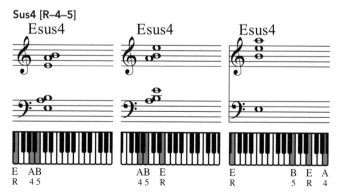

Esus4

E AB
R 4 5

Esus4

AB E
4 5 R

Esus4

E B E A
R 5 R 4

E

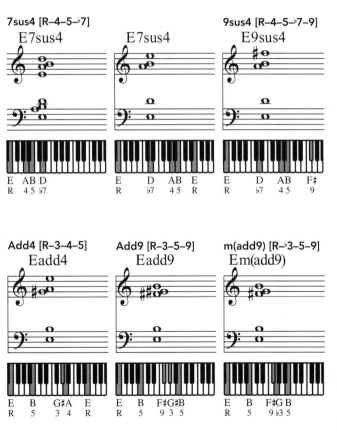

7sus4 [R–4–5–♭7]

E7sus4

E7sus4

E
R

AB D
4 5 ♭7

E
R

D
♭7

AB E
4 5 R

9sus4 [R–4–5–♭7–9]

E9sus4

E
R

D
♭7

AB F#
4 5 9

Add4 [R–3–4–5]

Eadd4

E
R

B
5

G#A E
3 4 R

Add9 [R–3–5–9]

Eadd9

E
R

B
5

F#G#B
9 3 5

m(add9) [R–♭3–5–9]

Em(add9)

E
R

B
5

F#G B
9♭3 5

F

Triads

Major [R–3–5]

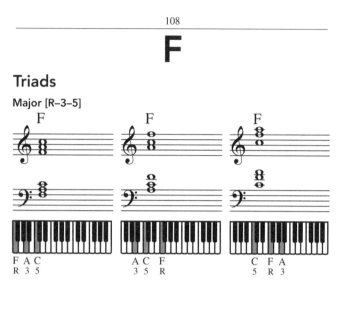

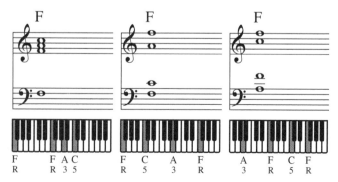

F

Minor (m, -) [R–♭3–5]

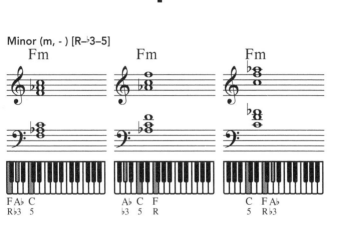

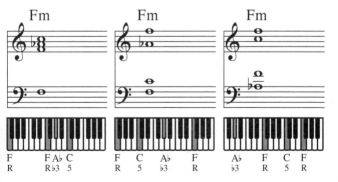

F

Diminished (°, dim) [R–♭3–♭5]

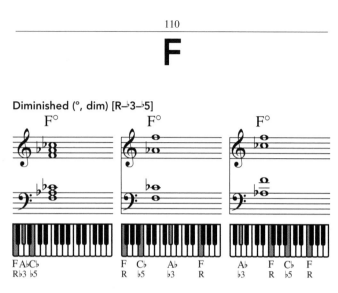

Augmented (+, aug) [R–3–♯5]

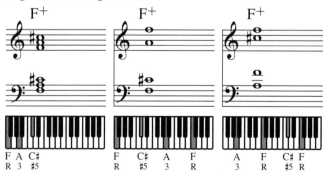

F

Seventh Chords

Dominant Seventh (7) [R–3–5–♭7]

F

Dominant Seventh Chords with Alterations

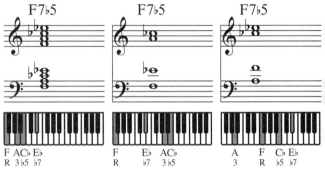

F7♭5   F7♭5   F7♭5

F A C♭ E♭
R 3 ♭5 ♭7

F   E♭   A C♭
R   ♭7   3 ♭5

A   F   C♭ E♭
3   R   ♭5 ♭7

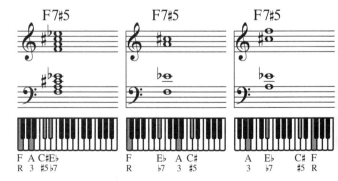

F7♯5   F7♯5   F7♯5

F A C♯ E♭
R 3 ♯5 ♭7

F   E♭   A C♯
R   ♭7   3 ♯5

A   E♭   C♯ F
3   ♭7   ♯5 R

F

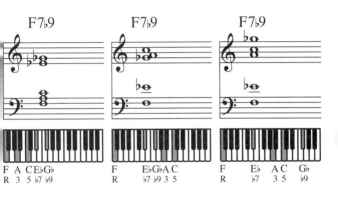

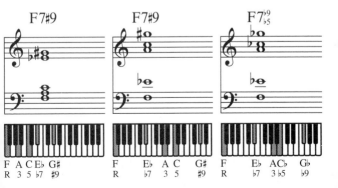

F

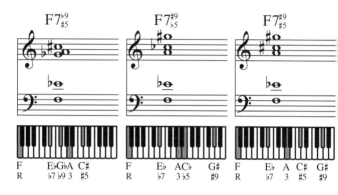

F7♭9#5

F		Eb Gb A	C#
R		b7 b9 3	#5

F7#9♭5

F	Eb	ACb	G#
R	b7	3 b5	#9

F7#9#5

F	Eb	A	C#	G#
R	b7	3	#5	#9

Major Seventh (maj7, M7, ma7, 7) [R–3–5–7]

Fmaj7

F	A	C	E
R	3	5	7

Fmaj7

A	C	EF
3	5	7R

Fmaj7

C	EF	A
5	7R	3

F

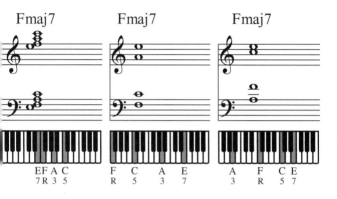

Fmaj7	Fmaj7	Fmaj7
EF A C	F C A E	A F C E
7R 3 5	R 5 3 7	3 R 5 7

Major Seventh Chords with Alterations

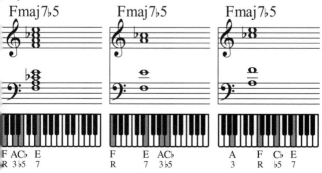

Fmaj7♭5	Fmaj7♭5	Fmaj7♭5
F AC♭ E	F E AC♭	A F C♭ E
R 3♭5 7	R 7 3♭5	3 R ♭5 7

F

Fmaj7#5   Fmaj7#5   Fmaj7#5

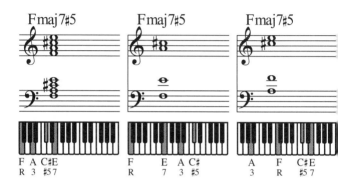

F A C#E
R 3 #57

F E A C#
R 7 3 #5

A F C#E
3 R #57

Minor Seventh (m7, min7, -7) [R–♭3–5–♭7]

Fm7   Fm7   Fm7

F A♭ CE♭
R ♭3 5 ♭7

A♭ CE♭F
♭3 5 ♭7 R

CE♭F A♭
5 ♭7 R ♭3

F

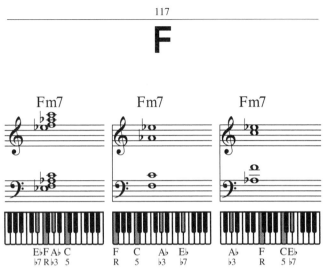

Fm7
Eb F Ab C
b7 R b3 5

Fm7
F C   Ab Eb
R 5   b3 b7

Fm7
Ab   F   C Eb
b3   R   5 b7

Minor Seventh Chords with Alterations

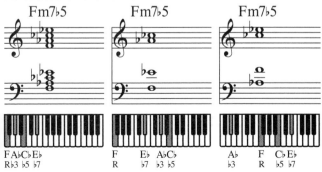

Fm7b5
F Ab Cb Eb
R b3 b5 b7

Fm7b5
F   Eb Ab Cb
R   b7 b3 b5

Fm7b5
Ab   F   Cb Eb
b3   R   b5 b7

F

Minor-Major Seventh [m(maj7), m/M7] [R–♭3–5–7]

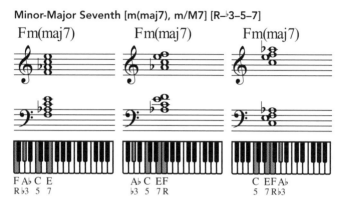

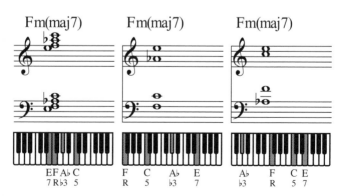

F

Diminished Seventh (°7) [R–♭3–♭5–♭♭7]

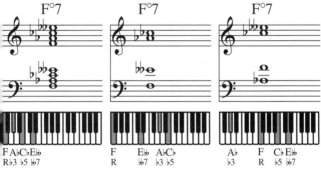

F°7 — F A♭ C♭ E♭♭ / R ♭3 ♭5 ♭♭7

F°7 — F E♭♭ A♭ C♭ / R ♭♭7 ♭3 ♭5

F°7 — A♭ F C♭ E♭♭ / ♭3 R ♭5 ♭♭7

Ninth Chords

Dominant Ninth (9) [R–3–5–♭7–9]

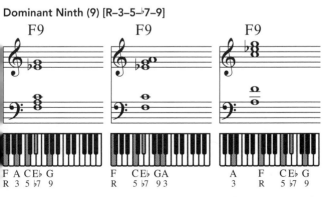

F9 — F A C E♭ G / R 3 5 ♭7 9

F9 — F C E♭ G A / R 5 ♭7 9 3

F9 — A F C E♭ G / 3 R 5 ♭7 9

F

Dominant Ninth Chords with Alterations

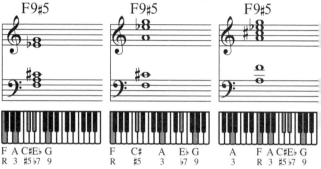

F9#5

F A C#Eb G
R 3 #5 b7 9

F9#5

F   C#   A   Eb G
R   #5   3   b7 9

F9#5

A   F A C#Eb G
3   R 3 #5 b7 9

Major Ninth (maj9, M9, ma9, 9) [R–3–5–7–9]

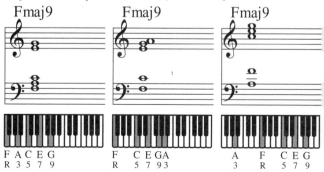

Fmaj9

F A C E G
R 3 5 7 9

Fmaj9

F   C E GA
R   5 7 93

Fmaj9

A   F   C E G
3   R   5 7 9

F

Minor Ninth (m9, min9, -9) [R–♭3–5–♭7–9]

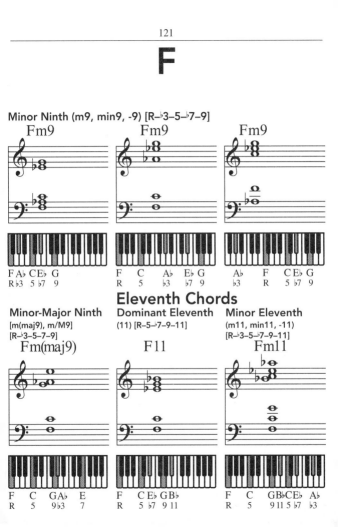

Fm9

Fm9

Fm9

F A♭ C E♭ G	F C A♭ E♭ G	A♭ F C E♭ G
R ♭3 5 ♭7 9	R 5 ♭3 ♭7 9	♭3 R 5 ♭7 9

Eleventh Chords

Minor-Major Ninth
[m(maj9), m/M9]
[R–3–5–7–9]

Dominant Eleventh
(11) [R–5–♭7–9–11]

Minor Eleventh
(m11, min11, -11)
[R–♭3–5–♭7–9–11]

Fm(maj9)

F11

Fm11

F C G A♭ E	F C E♭ G B♭	F C G B♭ C E♭ A♭
R 5 9 ♭3 7	R 5 ♭7 9 11	R 5 9 11 5 ♭7 ♭3

F

Thirteenth Chords

Dominant Thirteenth (13) [R–3–5–♭7–9–13]

Major Thirteenth (maj13, M13, ma13) [R–3–5–7–9–13]

Minor Thirteenth (m13, min13, -13) [R–♭3–5–♭7–9–11–13]

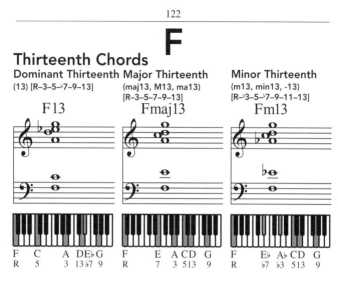

Sixth Chords

Sixth Chords (6) [R–3–5–6]

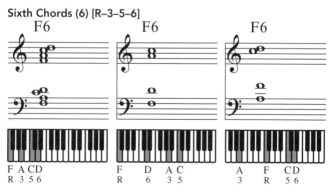

F

Six-Nine Chords ($^6_9$) [R–3–5–6–9]

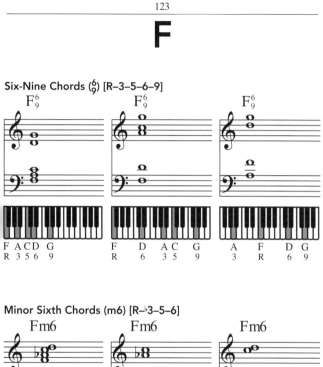

F^6_9 F^6_9 F^6_9

F A C D	G	F	D	A C	G	A	F	D G
R 3 5 6	9	R	6	3 5	9	3	R	6 9

Minor Sixth Chords (m6) [R–♭3–5–6]

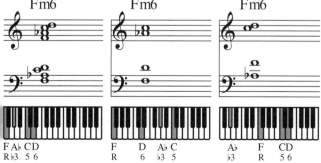

Fm6   Fm6   Fm6

F A♭ C D	F	D	A♭ C	A♭	F	C D
R ♭3 5 6	R	6	♭3 5	♭3	R	5 6

F

Minor Six-Nine Chords (m$_9^6$) [R–$\flat$3–5–6–9]

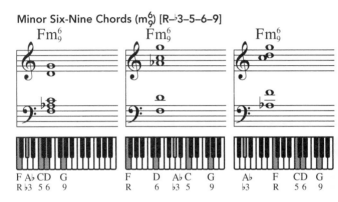

Power Chords ("5" Chords) [R–5]

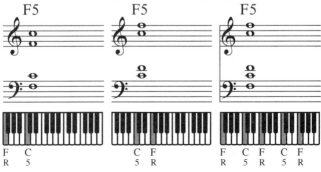

F

Suspended (sus) and add Chords

Sus2 [R–2–5]

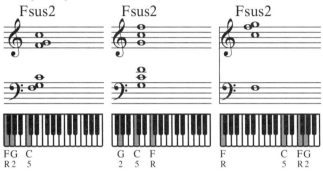

Fsus2

Fsus2

Fsus2

FG C
R 2 5

G C F
2 5 R

F
R

C FG
5 R 2

Sus4 [R–4–5]

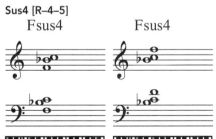

Fsus4

Fsus4

Fsus4

F Bb C
R 4 5

Bb C F
4 5 R

F
R

C F Bb
5 R 4

F

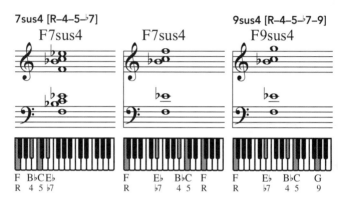

7sus4 [R–4–5–♭7]

F7sus4

F7sus4

9sus4 [R–4–5–♭7–9]

F9sus4

F   B♭C E♭
R   4 5 ♭7

F   E♭   B♭C   F
R   ♭7   4 5   R

F   E♭   B♭C   G
R   ♭7   4 5   9

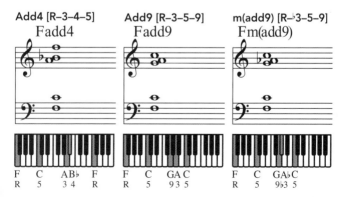

Add4 [R–3–4–5]

Fadd4

Add9 [R–3–5–9]

Fadd9

m(add9) [R–♭3–5–9]

Fm(add9)

F   C   A B♭   F
R   5   3 4   R

F   C   G A C
R   5   9 3 5

F   C   G A♭ C
R   5   9 ♭3 5

F♯/G♭

Triads
Major [R–3–5]

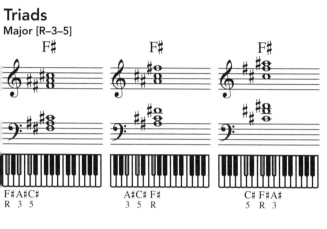

F♯   F♯   F♯

F♯A♯C♯   A♯C♯ F♯   C♯ F♯A♯
R 3 5   3 5 R   5 R 3

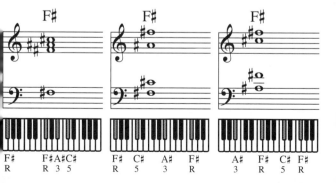

F♯   F♯   F♯

F♯   F♯A♯C♯   F♯ C♯ A♯   F♯   A♯ F♯ C♯ F♯
R   R 3 5   R 5   3   R   3   R 5 R

F#/Gb

Minor (m, -) [R–b3–5]

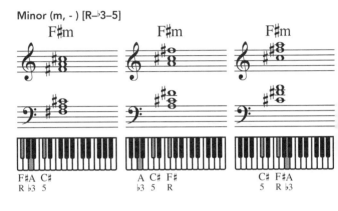

F#m   F#m   F#m

F#A C#   A C# F#   C# F#A
R b3 5   b3 5 R   5 R b3

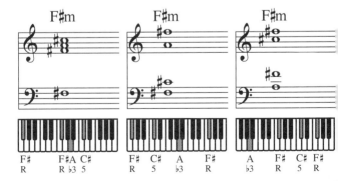

F#m   F#m   F#m

F#   F#A C#   F# C# A   F#   A   F# C# F#
R   R b3 5   R 5 b3   R   b3   R 5 R

F♯/G♭

Diminished (°, dim) [R–♭3–♭5]

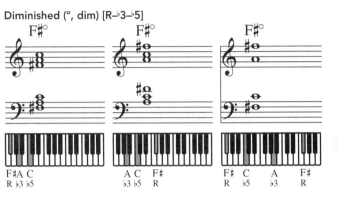

F♯°

F♯A C
R ♭3 ♭5

F♯°

A C F♯
♭3 ♭5 R

F♯°

F♯ C A F♯
R ♭5 ♭3 R

Augmented (+, aug) [R–3–♯5]

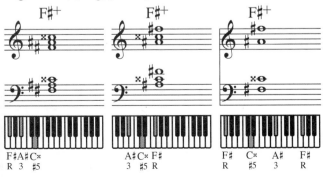

F♯+

F♯A♯C×
R 3 ♯5

F♯+

A♯C× F♯
3 ♯5 R

F♯+

F♯ C× A♯ F♯
R ♯5 3 R

F♯/G♭

Seventh Chords
Dominant Seventh (7) [R–3–5–♭7]

F♯7 — F♯A♯C♯E — R 3 5 ♭7

F♯7 — A♯C♯EF♯ — 3 5 ♭7R

F♯7 — C♯EF♯A♯ — 5 ♭7R 3

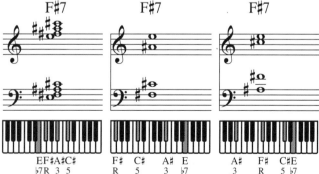

F♯7 — EF♯A♯C♯ — ♭7R 3 5

F♯7 — F♯ C♯ A♯ E — R 5 3 ♭7

F♯7 — A♯ F♯ C♯E — 3 R 5 ♭7

F#/Gb

Dominant Seventh Chords with Alterations

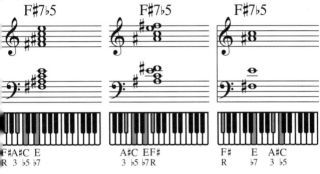

F#7b5

F#7b5

F#7b5

F#A#C E
R 3 b5 b7

A#C EF#
3 b5 b7 R

F#   E   A#C
R   b7   3 b5

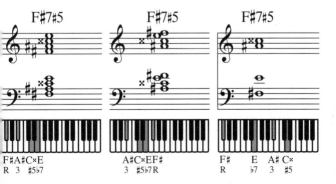

F#7#5

F#7#5

F#7#5

F#A#C×E
R 3 #5 b7

A#C×EF#
3 #5 b7 R

F#   E   A# C×
R   b7   3 #5

F#/G♭

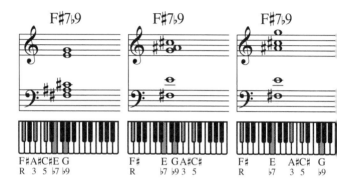

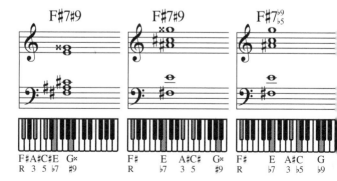

F♯/G♭

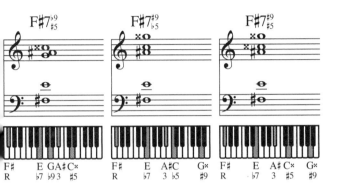

F♯7♭9♯5

F♯7♯9♭5

F♯7♯9♯5

| F♯ | E | G A♯ C× |
| R | ♭7 | ♭9 3 ♯5 |

| F♯ | E | A♯ C | G× |
| R | ♭7 | 3 ♭5 | ♯9 |

| F♯ | E | A♯ C× | G× |
| R | ♭7 | 3 ♯5 | ♯9 |

Major Seventh (maj7, M7, ma7, 7) [R–3–5–7]

F♯maj7

F♯maj7

F♯maj7

| F♯ A♯ C♯ E♯ |
| R 3 5 7 |

| A♯ C♯ E♯ F♯ |
| 3 5 7 R |

| C♯ E♯ F♯ A♯ |
| 5 7 R 3 |

F#/Gb

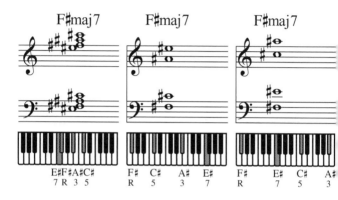

F#maj7
E#F#A#C#
7 R 3 5

F#maj7
F# C# A# E#
R 5 3 7

F#maj7
F# E# C# A#
R 7 5 3

Major Seventh Chords with Alterations

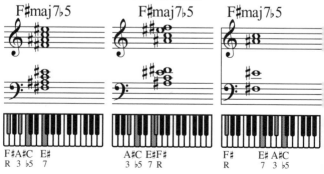

F#maj7b5
F#A#C E#
R 3 b5 7

F#maj7b5
A#C E#F#
3 b5 7 R

F#maj7b5
F# E# A#C
R 7 3 b5

F#/Gb

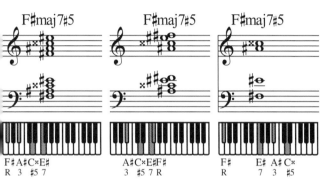

F#maj7#5   F#maj7#5   F#maj7#5

F#A#C×E#   A#C×E#F#   F#   E# A# C×
R 3 #5 7   3 #5 7 R   R   7 3 #5

Minor Seventh (m7, min7, -7) [R–b3–5–b7]

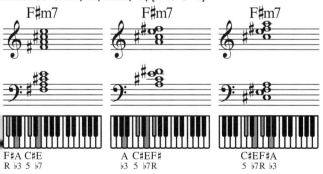

F#m7   F#m7   F#m7

F#A C#E   A C#EF#   C#EF#A
R b3 5 b7   b3 5 b7R   5 b7R b3

F♯/G♭

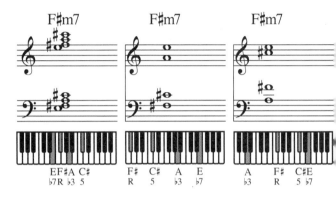

F♯m7

F♯m7

F♯m7

E F♯ A C♯
♭7 R ♭3 5

F♯ C♯ A E
R 5 ♭3 ♭7

A F♯ C♯ E
♭3 R 5 ♭7

Minor Seventh Chords with Alterations

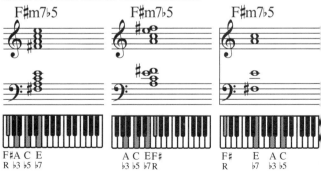

F♯m7♭5

F♯m7♭5

F♯m7♭5

F♯ A C E
R ♭3 ♭5 ♭7

A C E F♯
♭3 ♭5 ♭7 R

F♯ E A C
R ♭7 ♭3 ♭5

F♯/G♭

Minor-Major Seventh [m(maj7), m/M7] [R–♭3–5–7]

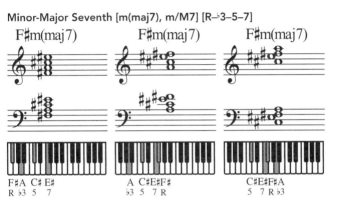

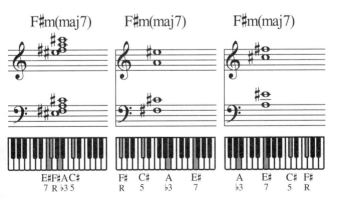

F#/G♭

Diminished Seventh (°7) [R–♭3–♭5–♭♭7]

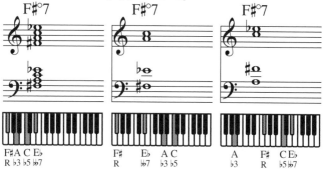

F#°7 | F#°7 | F#°7

F#A C E♭
R ♭3 ♭5 ♭♭7

F#   E♭   A C
R   ♭♭7   ♭3 ♭5

A   F#   C E♭
♭3   R   ♭5 ♭♭7

Ninth Chords

Dominant Ninth (9) [R–3–5–♭7–9]

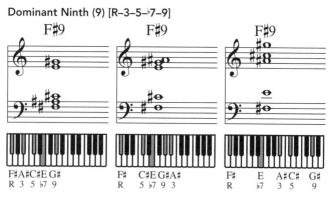

F#9 | F#9 | F#9

F#A C#E G#
R 3 5 ♭7 9

F#   C#E G#A#
R   5 ♭7 9 3

F#   E   A#C#   G#
R   ♭7   3 5   9

F#/Gb

Dominant Ninth Chords with Alterations

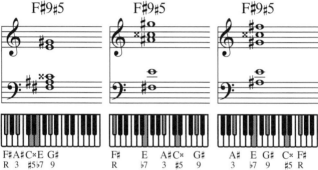

F#9#5   F#9#5   F#9#5

Major Ninth (maj9, M9, ma9, 9) [R–3–5–7–9]

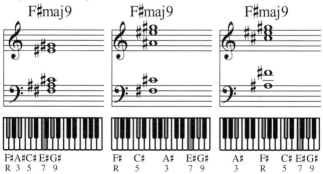

F#maj9   F#maj9   F#maj9

F♯/G♭

Minor Ninth (m9, min9, -9) [R–♭3–5–♭7–9]

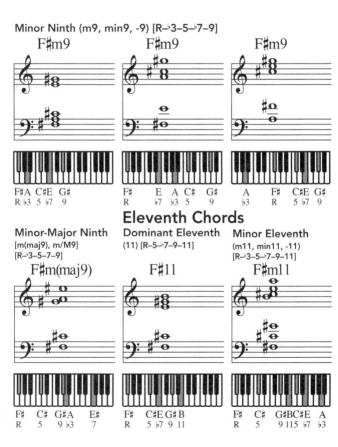

F♯m9

F♯m9

F♯m9

F♯A C♯E G♯
R ♭3 5 ♭7 9

F♯ E A C♯ G♯
R ♭7 ♭3 5 9

A F♯ C♯E G♯
♭3 R 5 ♭7 9

Eleventh Chords

Minor-Major Ninth
[m(maj9), m/M9]
[R–♭3–5–7–9]

Dominant Eleventh
(11) [R–5–♭7–9–11]

Minor Eleventh
(m11, min11, -11)
[R–♭3–5–♭7–9–11]

F♯m(maj9)

F♯11

F♯m11

F♯ C♯ G♯A E♯
R 5 9 ♭3 7

F♯ C♯E G♯ B
R 5 ♭7 9 11

F♯ C♯ G♯BC♯E A
R 5 9 11 5 ♭7 ♭3

F♯/G♭

Thirteenth Chords

Dominant Thirteenth
(13) [R–3–5–♭7–9–13]

Major Thirteenth
(maj13, M13, ma13)
[R–3–5–7–9–13]

Minor Thirteenth
(m13, min13, -13)
[R–♭3–5–♭7–9–11–13]

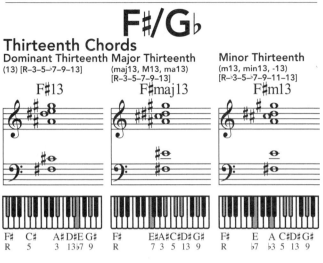

F♯13

F♯maj13

F♯m13

F♯ C♯   A♯ D♯ E G♯
R   5   3 13 ♭7 9

F♯   E♯A♯C♯D♯ G♯
R   7 3 5 13 9

F♯   E A C♯D♯ G♯
R   ♭7 ♭3 5 13 9

Sixth Chords

Sixth Chords (6) [R–3–5–6]

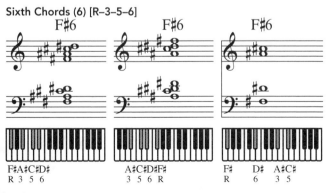

F♯6

F♯6

F♯6

F♯A♯C♯D♯
R 3 5 6

A♯C♯D♯F♯
3 5 6 R

F♯   D♯ A♯C♯
R   6   3 5

F#/Gb

Six-Nine Chords (6/9) [R–3–5–6–9]

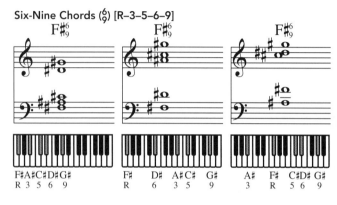

F#6/9

F#A#C#D#G#
R 3 5 6 9

F#6/9

F#　D#　A#C#　G#
R　　6　　3 5　　9

F#6/9

A#　F#　C#D#　G#
3　　R　　5 6　　9

Minor Sixth Chords (m6) [R–b3–5–6]

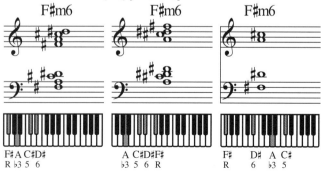

F#m6

F#A C#D#
R b3 5 6

F#m6

A C#D#F#
b3 5 6 R

F#m6

F#　D#　A C#
R　　6　　b3 5

F#/Gb

Minor Six-Nine Chords (m⁶₉) [R–b3–5–6–9]

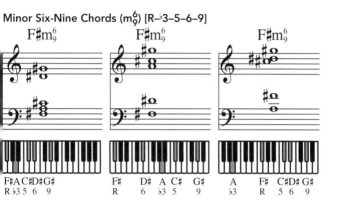

Power Chords ("5" Chords) [R–5]

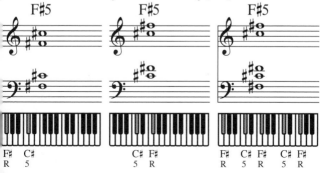

F#/G♭

Suspended (sus) and add Chords

Sus2 [R–2–5]

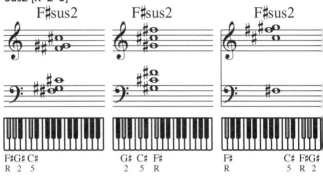

F#sus2   F#sus2   F#sus2

F#G# C#
R 2 5

G# C# F#
2 5 R

F#
R   C# F#G#
5 R 2

Sus4 [R–4–5]

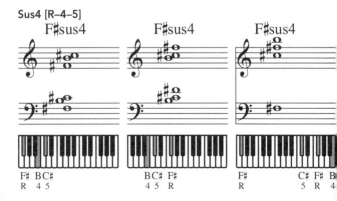

F#sus4   F#sus4   F#sus4

F# BC#
R 4 5

BC# F#
4 5 R

F#
R   C# F# B
5 R 4

F#/Gb

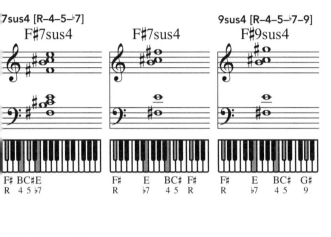

7sus4 [R–4–5–♭7]
F#7sus4

F#7sus4

9sus4 [R–4–5–♭7–9]
F#9sus4

F# BC#E
R 4 5 ♭7

F#   E   BC# F#
R   ♭7   4 5 R

F#   E   BC# G#
R   ♭7   4 5   9

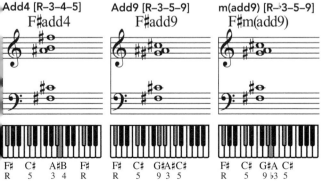

Add4 [R–3–4–5]
F#add4

Add9 [R–3–5–9]
F#add9

m(add9) [R–♭3–5–9]
F#m(add9)

F#   C#   A#B   F#
R   5   3 4   R

F#   C#   G#A#C#
R   5   9 3 5

F#   C#   G#A C#
R   5   9 ♭3 5

G

Triads

Major [R–3–5]

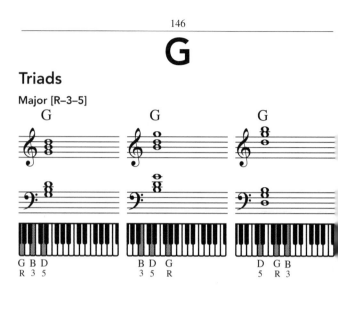

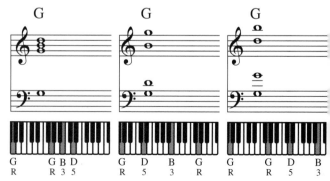

G

Minor (m, -) [R–♭3–5]

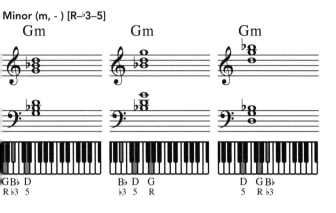

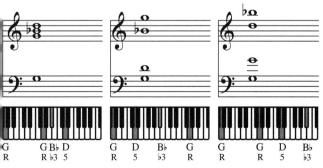

G

Diminished (°, dim) [R–♭3–♭5]

Augmented (+, aug) [R–3–♯5]

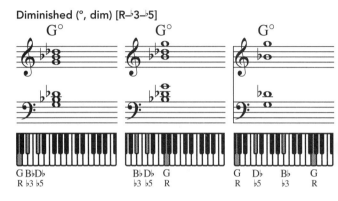

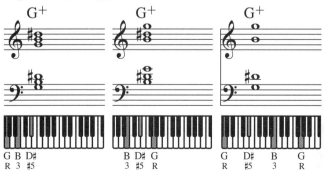

G

Seventh Chords

Dominant Seventh (7) [R–3–5–♭7]

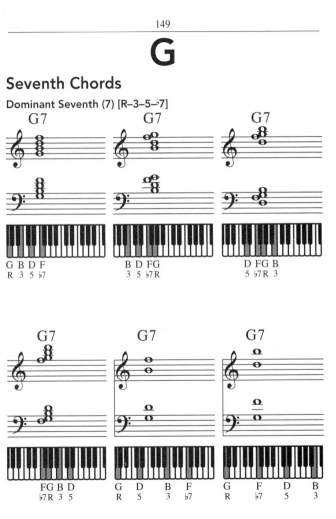

G

Dominant Seventh Chords with Alterations

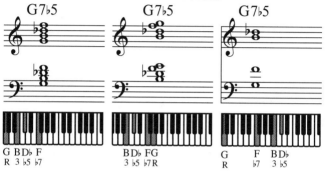

G7♭5

G7♭5

G7♭5

G B D♭ F
R 3 ♭5 ♭7

B D♭ F G
3 ♭5 ♭7 R

G   F   B D♭
R   ♭7 3 ♭5

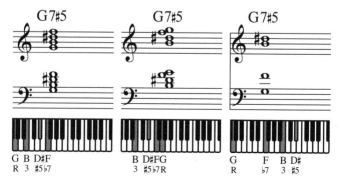

G7♯5

G7♯5

G7♯5

G B D♯ F
R 3 ♯5 7

B D♯ F G
3 ♯5 ♭7 R

G   F   B D♯
R   ♭7 3 ♯5

G

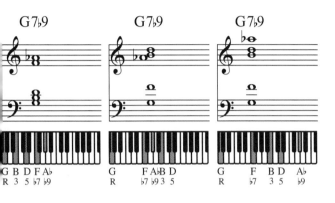

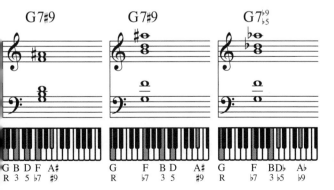

G

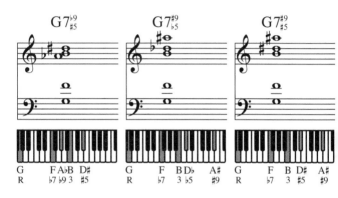

$G7^{\flat9}_{\sharp5}$ $G7^{\sharp9}_{\flat5}$ $G7^{\sharp9}_{\sharp5}$

| G | | F | A♭ | B | D♯ | | G | | F | B | D♭ | A♯ | | G | | F | B | D♯ | A♯ |
| R | | ♭7 | ♭9 | 3 | ♯5 | | R | | ♭7 | 3 | ♭5 | ♯9 | | R | | ♭7 | 3 | ♯5 | ♯9 |

Major Seventh (maj7, M7, ma7, 7) [R–3–5–7]

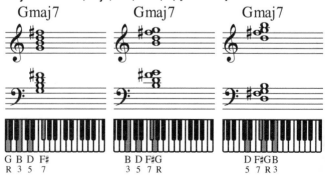

Gmaj7   Gmaj7   Gmaj7

| G | B | D | F♯ | | B | D | F♯ | G | | D | F♯ | G | B |
| R | 3 | 5 | 7 | | 3 | 5 | 7 | R | | 5 | 7 | R | 3 |

G

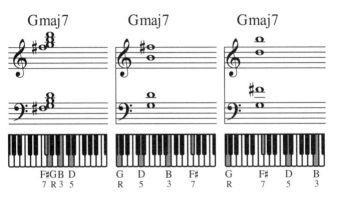

Gmaj7

F#GB D
7 R 3 5

Gmaj7

G D B F#
R 5 3 7

Gmaj7

G F# D B
R 7 5 3

Major Seventh Chords with Alterations

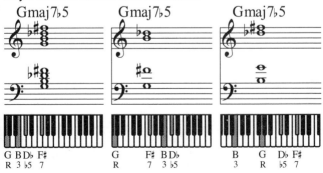

Gmaj7♭5

G B D♭ F#
R 3 ♭5 7

Gmaj7♭5

G F# B D♭
R 7 3 ♭5

Gmaj7♭5

B G D♭ F#
3 R ♭5 7

G

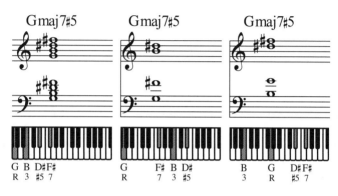

Gmaj7#5

G B D#F#
R 3 #5 7

Gmaj7#5

G   F# B D#
R   7 3 #5

Gmaj7#5

B   G   D#F#
3   R   #5 7

Minor Seventh (m7, min7, -7) [R–♭3–5–♭7]

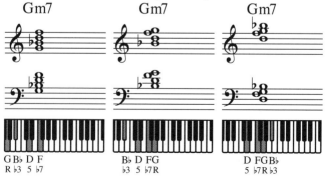

Gm7

G B♭ D F
R ♭3 5 ♭7

Gm7

B♭ D FG
♭3 5 ♭7R

Gm7

D FGB♭
5 ♭7R ♭3

G

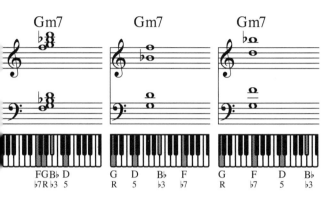

Gm7	Gm7	Gm7

FGBb D
b7R b3 5

G D Bb F
R 5 b3 b7

G F D Bb
R b7 5 b3

Minor Seventh Chords with Alterations

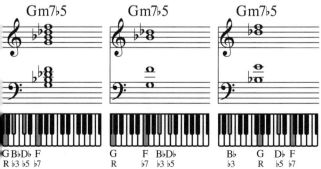

Gm7b5	Gm7b5	Gm7b5

GBbDb F
R b3 b5 b7

G F BbDb
R b7 b3 b5

Bb G Db F
b3 R b5 b7

G

Minor-Major Seventh [m(maj7), m/M7] [R–♭3–5–7]

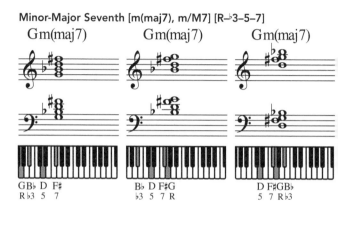

Gm(maj7)	Gm(maj7)	Gm(maj7)
G B♭ D F#	B♭ D F# G	D F# G B♭
R ♭3 5 7	♭3 5 7 R	5 7 R ♭3

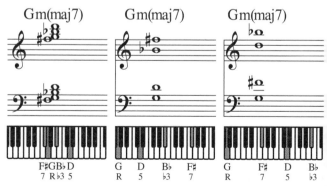

Gm(maj7)	Gm(maj7)	Gm(maj7)
F# G B♭ D	G D B♭ F#	G F# D B♭
7 R ♭3 5	R 5 ♭3 7	R 7 5 ♭3

G

Diminished Seventh (°7) [R–♭3–♭5–♭♭7]

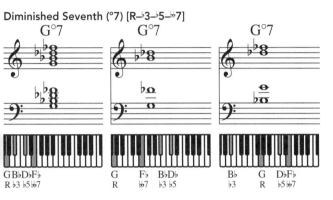

Ninth Chords

Dominant Ninth (9) [R–3–5–♭7–9]

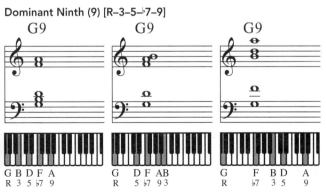

G

Dominant Ninth Chords with Alterations

G9#5   G9#5   G9#5

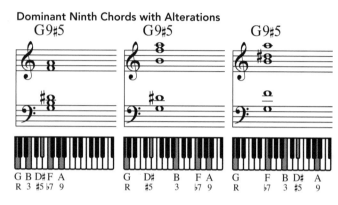

G B D# F A
R 3 #5 b7 9

G   D#   B   F A
R   #5   3   b7 9

G   F   B D#   A
R   b7   3 #5   9

Major Ninth (maj9, M9, ma9, 9) [R–3–5–7–9]

Gmaj9   Gmaj9   Gmaj9

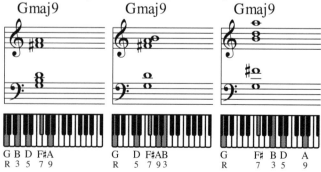

G B D F# A
R 3 5 7 9

G   D F#AB
R   5 793

G   F# B D   A
R   7 3 5   9

G

Minor Ninth (m9, min9, -9) [R–♭3–5–♭7–9]

Gm9   Gm9   Gm9

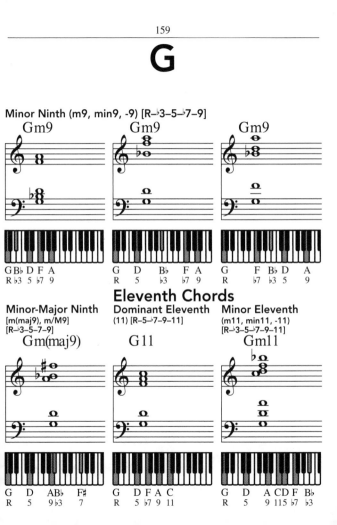

G B♭ D F A   G   D   B♭   F A   G   F B♭ D   A
R ♭3 5 ♭7 9   R   5   ♭3   ♭7 9   R   ♭7 ♭3 5   9

Eleventh Chords

Minor-Major Ninth   **Dominant Eleventh**   **Minor Eleventh**
[m(maj9), m/M9]   (11) [R–5–♭7–9–11]   (m11, min11, -11)
[R–♭3–5–7–9]   [R–♭3–5–♭7–9–11]

Gm(maj9)   G11   Gm11

G   D   A B♭   F♯   G   D F A   C   G   D   A C D F   B♭
R   5   9 ♭3   7   R   5 ♭7 9   11   R   5   9 11 5 ♭7   ♭3

G

Thirteenth Chords

Dominant Thirteenth
(13) [R–3–5–♭7–9–13]

Major Thirteenth
(maj13, M13, ma13)
[R–3–5–7–9–13]

Minor Thirteenth
(m13, min13, -13)
[R–♭3–5–♭7–9–11–13]

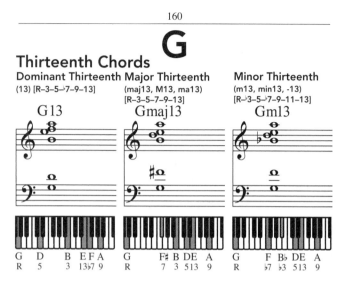

G13

Gmaj13

Gm13

G13	Gmaj13	Gm13
G D B E F A	G F# B D E A	G F B♭ D E A
R 5 3 13 ♭7 9	R 7 3 5 13 9	R ♭7 ♭3 5 13 9

Sixth Chords

Sixth Chords (6) [R–3–5–6]

G6

G6

G6

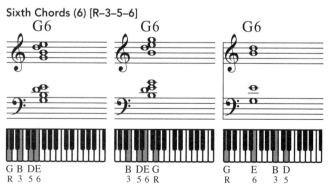

G6	G6	G6
G B D E	B D E G	G E B D
R 3 5 6	3 5 6 R	R 6 3 5

G

Six-Nine Chords ($^6_9$) [R–3–5–6–9]

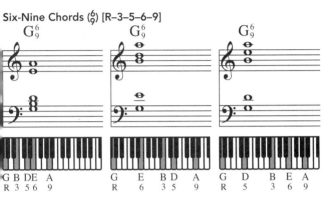

G^6_9 — G B D E A / R 3 5 6 9

G^6_9 — G E B D A / R 6 3 5 9

G^6_9 — G D B E A / R 5 3 6 9

Minor Sixth Chords (m6) [R–♭3–5–6]

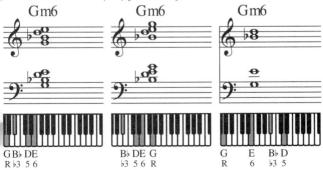

Gm6 — G B♭ D E / R ♭3 5 6

Gm6 — B♭ D E G / ♭3 5 6 R

Gm6 — G E B♭ D / R 6 ♭3 5

G

Minor Six-Nine Chords (m⁶₉) [R–♭3–5–6–9]

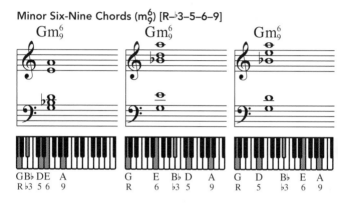

Gm⁶₉					Gm⁶₉					Gm⁶₉				
G	B♭	D	E	A	G	E	B♭	D	A	G	D	B♭	E	A
R	♭3	5	6	9	R	6	♭3	5	9	R	5	♭3	6	9

Power Chords ("5" Chords) [R–5]

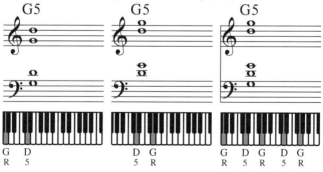

G5			G5			G5				
G	D		D	G		G	D	G	D	G
R	5		5	R		R	5	R	5	R

G

Suspended (sus) and add Chords

Sus2 [R–2–5]

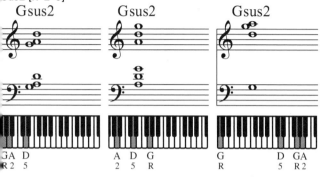

Gsus2

GA D
R 2 5

Gsus2

A   D   G
2   5   R

Gsus2

G   D   GA
R   5   R 2

Sus4 [R–4–5]

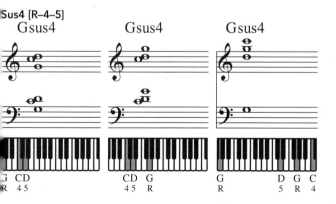

Gsus4

G CD
R 4 5

Gsus4

CD G
4 5 R

Gsus4

G   D   G   C
R   5   R   4

G

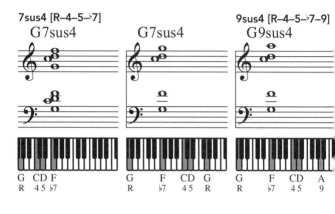

7sus4 [R–4–5–♭7]
G7sus4

G7sus4

9sus4 [R–4–5–♭7–9]
G9sus4

G	CD	F		G	F	CD	G		G	F	CD	A
R	45	♭7		R	♭7	45	R		R	♭7	45	9

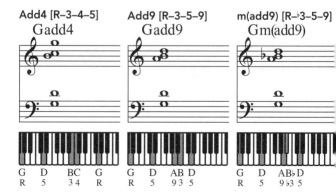

Add4 [R–3–4–5]
Gadd4

Add9 [R–3–5–9]
Gadd9

m(add9) [R–♭3–5–9]
Gm(add9)

G	D	BC	G		G	D	AB	D		G	D	AB♭	D
R	5	34	R		R	5	93	5		R	5	9♭3	5

G♯/A♭

Triads

Major [R–3–5]

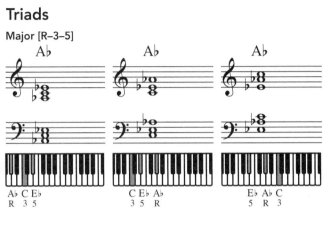

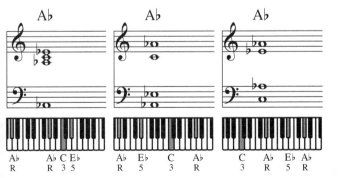

G#/Ab

Minor (m, -) [R–b3–5]

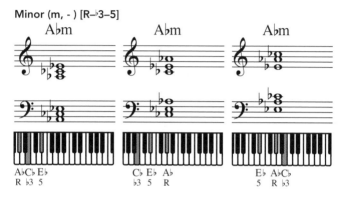

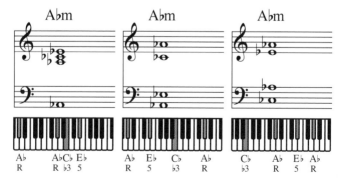

G♯/A♭

Diminished (°, dim) [R–♭3–♭5]

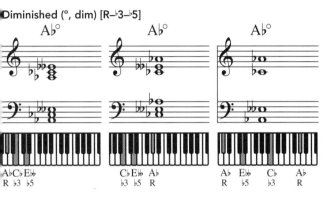

Augmented (+, aug) [R–3–♯5]

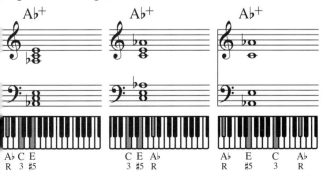

G♯/A♭

Seventh Chords

Dominant Seventh (7) [R–3–5–♭7]

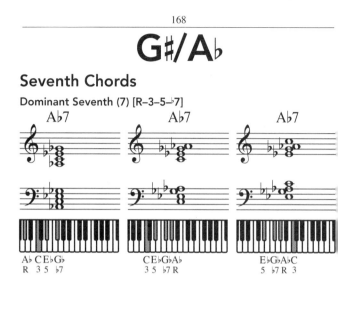

A♭7

A♭7

A♭7

A♭ C E♭ G♭
R 3 5 ♭7

C E♭ G♭ A♭
3 5 ♭7 R

E♭ G♭ A♭ C
5 ♭7 R 3

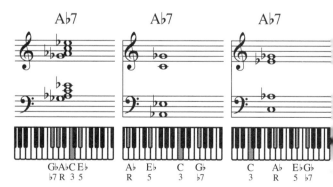

A♭7

A♭7

A♭7

G♭ A♭ C E♭
♭7 R 3 5

A♭   E♭   C   G♭
R   5   3   ♭7

C   A♭   E♭ G♭
3   R   5 ♭7

G#/Ab

Dominant Seventh Chords with Alterations

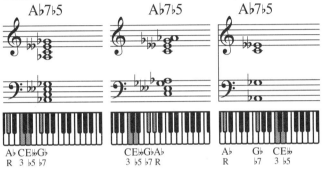

Ab7b5 — Ab CEbbGb — R 3 b5 b7

Ab7b5 — CEbbGbAb — 3 b5 b7 R

Ab7b5 — Ab Gb CEbb — R b7 3 b5

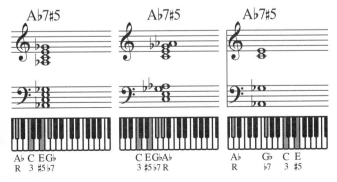

Ab7#5 — Ab C EGb — R 3 #5 b7

Ab7#5 — C EGbAb — 3 #5 b7 R

Ab7#5 — Ab Gb C E — R b7 3 #5

G♯/A♭

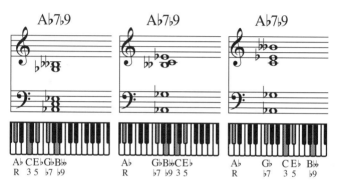

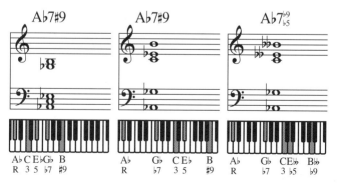

G♯/A♭

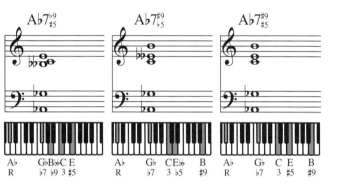

$A♭7^{♭9}_{♯5}$

A♭   G♭B♭♭C E
R   ♭7 ♭9 3 ♯5

$A♭7^{♯9}_{♭5}$

A♭   G♭   CE♭♭   B
R   ♭7   3 ♭5   ♯9

$A♭7^{♯9}_{♯5}$

A♭   G♭   C E   B
R   ♭7   3 ♯5   ♯9

Major Seventh (maj7, M7, ma7, 7) [R–3–5–7]

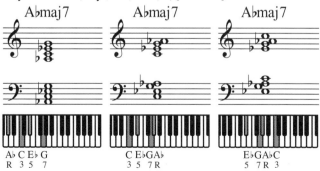

A♭maj7

A♭ C E♭ G
R 3 5 7

A♭maj7

C E♭GA♭
3 5 7R

A♭maj7

E♭GA♭C
5 7R 3

G♯/A♭

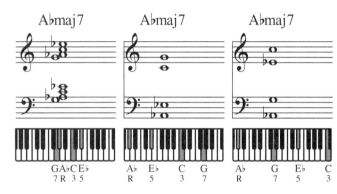

A♭maj7	A♭maj7	A♭maj7
G A♭ C E♭	A♭ E♭ C G	A♭ G E♭ C
7 R 3 5	R 5 3 7	R 7 5 3

Major Seventh Chords with Alterations

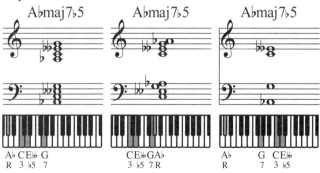

A♭maj7♭5	A♭maj7♭5	A♭maj7♭5
A♭ C E♭ G	C E♭ G A♭	A♭ G C E♭
R 3 ♭5 7	3 ♭5 7 R	R 7 3 ♭5

G♯/A♭

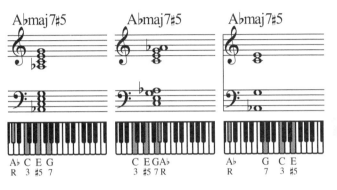

Abmaj7#5   Abmaj7#5   Abmaj7#5

A♭ C E G
R 3 #5 7

C E G A♭
3 #5 7 R

A♭   G C E
R   7 3 #5

Minor Seventh (m7, min7, -7) [R–♭3–5–♭7]

A♭m7   A♭m7   A♭m7

A♭ C♭ E♭ G♭
R ♭3 5 ♭7

C♭ E♭ G♭ A♭
♭3 5 ♭7 R

E♭ G♭ A♭ C♭
5 ♭7 R ♭3

G♯/A♭

A♭m7　　　　A♭m7　　　　A♭m7

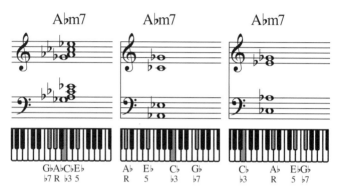

G♭A♭C♭E♭　　　A♭　E♭　C♭　G♭　　　C♭　　A♭　E♭G♭
♭7 R ♭3 5　　　R　5　♭3　♭7　　　♭3　　R　5 ♭7

Minor Seventh Chords with Alterations

A♭m7♭5　　　　A♭m7♭5　　　　A♭m7♭5

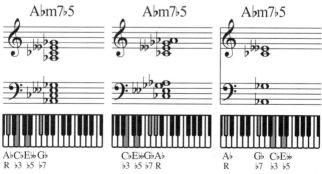

A♭C♭E♭♭G♭　　　C♭E♭♭G♭A♭　　　A♭　　G♭　C♭E♭♭
R ♭3 ♭5 ♭7　　　♭3 ♭5 ♭7 R　　　R　　♭7　♭3 ♭5

G♯/A♭

Minor-Major Seventh [m(maj7), m/M7] [R–♭3–5–7]

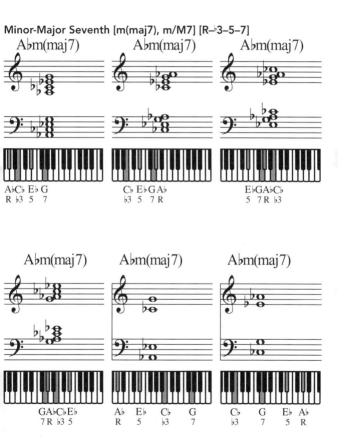

A♭m(maj7) A♭m(maj7) A♭m(maj7)

A♭ C♭ E♭ G
R ♭3 5 7

C♭ E♭ G A♭
♭3 5 7 R

E♭ G A♭ C♭
5 7 R ♭3

A♭m(maj7) A♭m(maj7) A♭m(maj7)

G A♭ C♭ E♭
7 R ♭3 5

A♭ E♭ C♭ G
R   5   ♭3 7

C♭ G E♭ A♭
♭3 7 5 R

G♯/A♭

Diminished Seventh (°7) [R–♭3–♭5–♭♭7]

A♭°7	A♭°7	A♭°7

A♭ C♭ E♭♭ G♭♭	A♭	G♭♭ C♭ E♭♭	C♭	A♭	E♭♭ G♭♭
R ♭3 ♭5 ♭♭7	R	♭♭7 ♭3 ♭5	♭3	R	♭5 ♭♭7

Ninth Chords

Dominant Ninth (9) [R–3–5–♭7–9]

A♭9	A♭9	A♭9

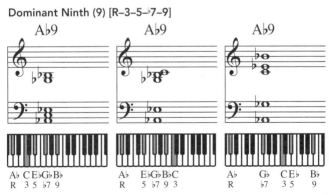

A♭ C E♭ G♭ B♭	A♭	E♭ G♭ B♭ C	A♭	G♭	C E♭	B♭
R 3 5 ♭7 9	R	5 ♭7 9 3	R	♭7	3 5	9

G♯/A♭

Dominant Ninth Chords with Alterations

A♭9♯5

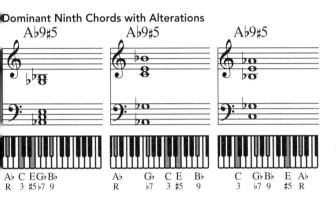

A♭ C E G♭ B♭
R 3 ♯5 ♭7 9

A♭9♯5

A♭   G♭   C E   B♭
R   ♭7   3 ♯5   9

A♭9♯5

C   G♭ B♭   E   A♭
3   ♭7 9   ♯5   R

Major Ninth (maj9, M9, ma9, 9) [R–3–5–7–9]

A♭maj9

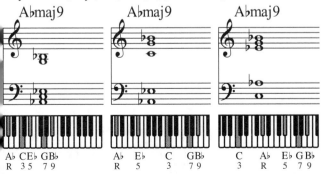

A♭ C E♭   G B♭
R 3 5   7 9

A♭maj9

A♭   E♭   C   G B♭
R   5   3   7 9

A♭maj9

C   A♭   E♭ G B♭
3   R   5 7 9

G♯/A♭

Minor Ninth (m9, min9, -9) [R–♭3–5–♭7–9]

A♭m9

A♭m9

A♭m9

A♭ C♭ E♭ G♭ B♭
R ♭3 5 ♭7 9

A♭   G♭ C♭ E♭   B♭
R   ♭7 ♭3 5   9

C♭   A♭   E♭ G♭ B♭
♭3   R   5 ♭7 9

Eleventh Chords

Minor-Major Ninth
[m(maj9), m/M9]
[R–♭3–5–7–9]

Dominant Eleventh
(11) [R–5–♭7–9–11]

Minor Eleventh
(m11, min11, -11)
[R–♭3–5–♭7–9–11]

A♭m(maj9)

A♭11

A♭m11

A♭   E♭   B♭ C♭   G
R   5   9 ♭3   7

A♭   E♭ G♭ B♭ D♭
R   5 ♭7 9 11

A♭   E♭   B♭ D♭ E♭ G♭ C♭
R   5   9 11 5 ♭7 ♭3

G#/A♭

Thirteenth Chords

Dominant Thirteenth
(13) [R–3–5–♭7–9–13]

Major Thirteenth
(maj13, M13, ma13)
[R–3–5–7–9–13]

Minor Thirteenth
(m13, min13, -13)
[R–♭3–5–♭7–9–11–13]

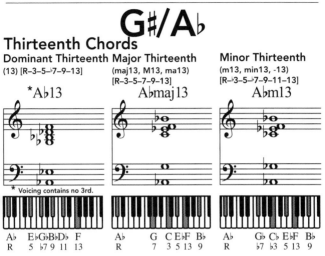

*A♭13

A♭maj13

A♭m13

* Voicing contains no 3rd.

A♭	E♭ G♭ B♭ D♭	F
R	5 ♭7 9 11	13

A♭	G C E♭ F B♭
R	7 3 5 13 9

A♭	G♭ C♭ E♭ F B♭
R	♭7 ♭3 5 13 9

Sixth Chords

Sixth Chords (6) [R–3–5–6]

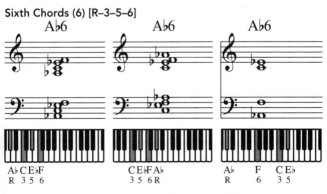

A♭6

A♭6

A♭6

A♭ C E♭ F
R 3 5 6

C E♭ F A♭
3 5 6 R

A♭	F	C E♭
R	6	3 5

G♯/A♭

Six-Nine Chords (⁶₉) [R–3–5–6–9]

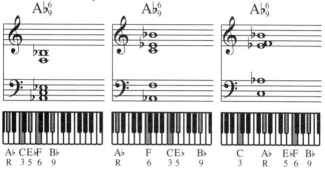

$A\flat^6_9$ $A\flat^6_9$ $A\flat^6_9$

A♭	C E♭ F	B♭
R	3 5 6	9

A♭	F	C E♭	B♭
R	6	3 5	9

C	A♭	E♭ F	B♭
3	R	5 6	9

Minor Sixth Chords (m6) [R–♭3–5–6]

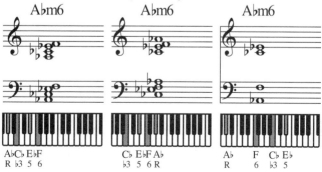

A♭m6   A♭m6   A♭m6

A♭ C♭ E♭ F
R ♭3 5 6

C♭ E♭ F A♭
♭3 5 6 R

A♭	F	C♭ E♭
R	6	♭3 5

G♯/A♭

Minor Six-Nine Chords (m⁶₉) [R–♭3–5–6–9]

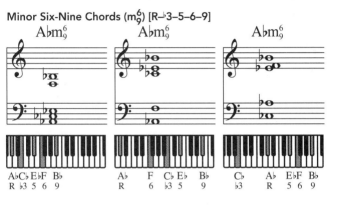

Power Chords ("5" Chords) [R–5]

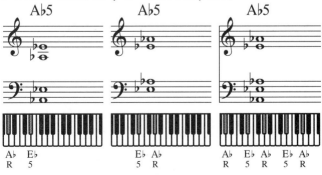

G♯/A♭

Suspended (sus) and add Chords

Sus2 [R–2–5]

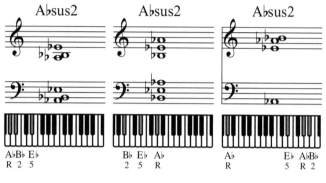

A♭ B♭ E♭	B♭ E♭ A♭	A♭ E♭ A♭ B♭
R 2 5	2 5 R	R 5 R 2

Sus4 [R–4–5]

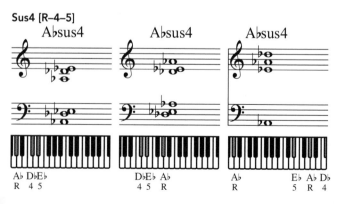

A♭ D♭ E♭	D♭ E♭ A♭	A♭ E♭ A♭ D♭
R 4 5	4 5 R	R 5 R 4

G♯/A♭

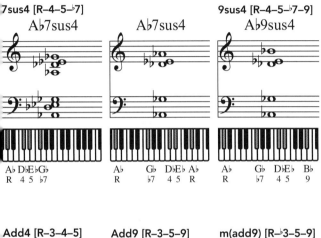

7sus4 [R–4–5–♭7]
A♭7sus4

A♭7sus4

9sus4 [R–4–5–♭7–9]
A♭9sus4

A♭ D♭E♭♭G♭
R 4 5 ♭7

A♭　　G♭ D♭E♭ A♭
R　　♭7 4 5 R

A♭　　G♭ D♭E♭　B♭
R　　♭7 4 5　9

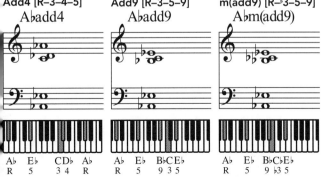

Add4 [R–3–4–5]
A♭add4

Add9 [R–3–5–9]
A♭add9

m(add9) [R–♭3–5–9]
A♭m(add9)

A♭　E♭　CD♭　A♭
R　5　3 4　R

A♭　E♭　B♭CE♭
R　5　9 3 5

A♭　E♭　B♭C♭E♭
R　5　9 ♭3 5

A

Triads

Major [R–3–5]

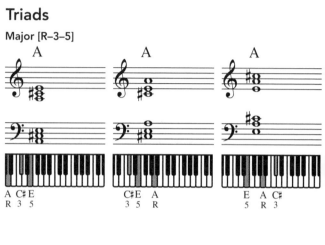

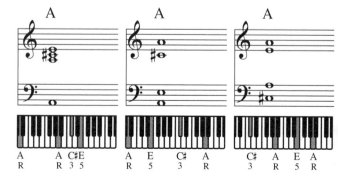

A

Minor (m, -) [R–♭3–5]

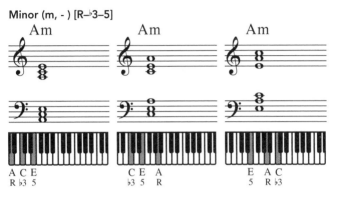

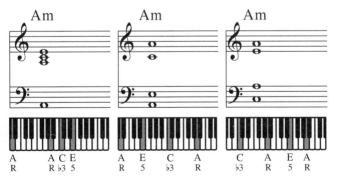

A

Diminished (°, dim) [R–♭3–♭5]

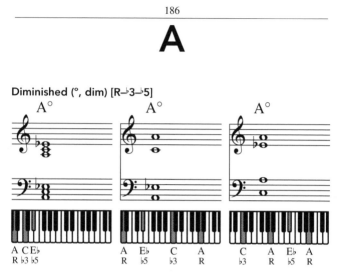

Augmented (+, aug) [R–3–♯5]

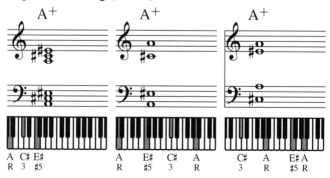

A

Seventh Chords

Dominant Seventh (7) [R–3–5–♭7]

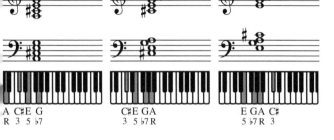

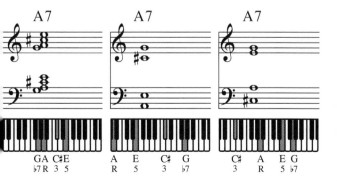

A

Dominant Seventh Chords with Alterations

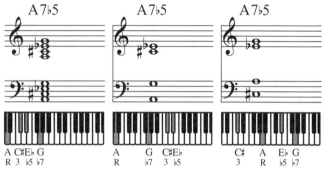

A7♭5   A7♭5   A7♭5

A C♯E♭ G   A   G   C♯E♭   C♯   A   E♭ G
R 3 ♭5 ♭7   R   ♭7   3 ♭5   3   R   ♭5 ♭7

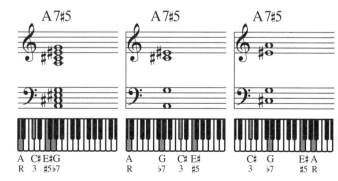

A7♯5   A7♯5   A7♯5

A C♯ E♯G   A   G   C♯ E♯   C♯   G   E♯ A
R 3 ♯5♭7   R   ♭7   3 ♯5   3   ♭7   ♯5 R

A

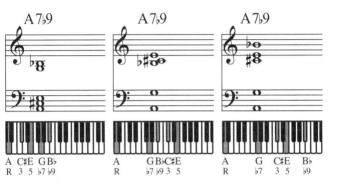

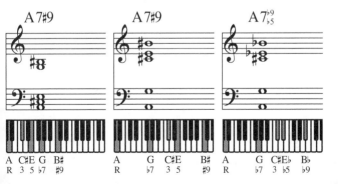

A

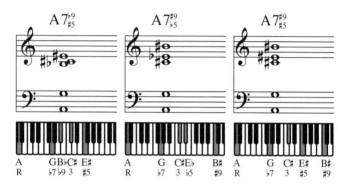

$A7^{\flat9}_{\sharp5}$

A   G B♭ C♯ E♯
R   ♭7 ♭9 3   ♯5

$A7^{\sharp9}_{\flat5}$

A   G   C♯ E♭   B♯
R   ♭7   3 ♭5   ♯9

$A7^{\sharp9}_{\sharp5}$

A   G   C♯ E♯   B♯
R   ♭7   3 ♯5   ♯9

Major Seventh (maj7, M7, ma7, 7) [R–3–5–7]

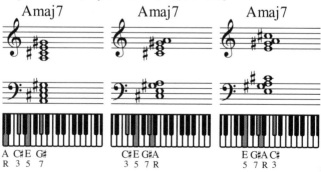

Amaj7

A C♯ E G♯
R 3 5 7

Amaj7

C♯ E G♯ A
3 5 7 R

Amaj7

E G♯ A C♯
5 7 R 3

A

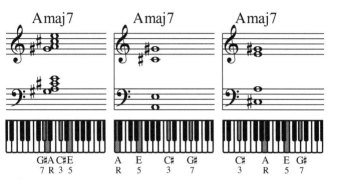

Major Seventh Chords with Alterations

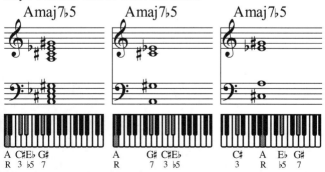

A

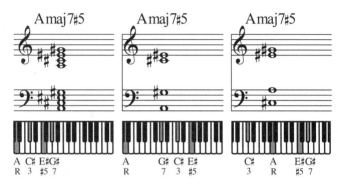

Amaj7#5

A C# E#G#
R 3 #5 7

Amaj7#5

A   G# C# E#
R   7 3 #5

Amaj7#5

C# A   E#G#
3 R   #5 7

Minor Seventh (m7, min7, -7) [R–♭3–5–♭7]

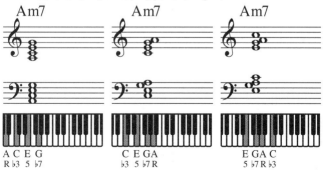

Am7

A C E G
R ♭3 5 ♭7

Am7

C E G A
♭3 5 ♭7 R

Am7

E G A C
5 ♭7 R ♭3

A

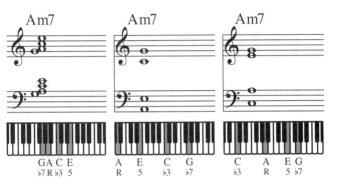

Minor Seventh Chords with Alterations

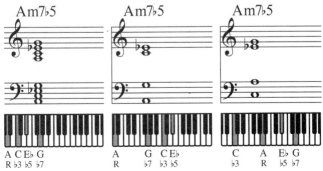

A

Minor-Major Seventh [m(maj7), m/M7] [R–♭3–5–7]

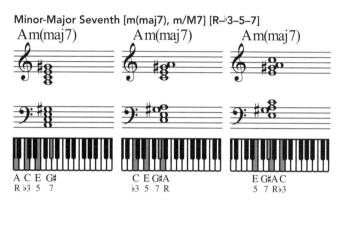

Am(maj7)
A C E G#
R ♭3 5 7

Am(maj7)
C E G#A
♭3 5 7 R

Am(maj7)
E G#A C
5 7 R♭3

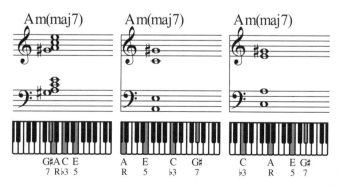

Am(maj7)
G#A C E
7 R♭3 5

Am(maj7)
A E C G#
R 5 ♭3 7

Am(maj7)
C A E G#
♭3 R 5 7

A

Diminished Seventh (°7) [R–♭3–♭5–♭♭7]

A°7   A°7   A°7

Ninth Chords

Dominant Ninth (9) [R–3–5–♭7–9]

A9   A9   A9

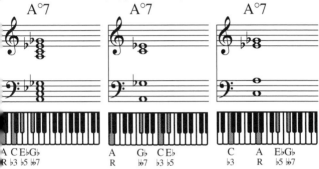

A

Dominant Ninth Chords with Alterations

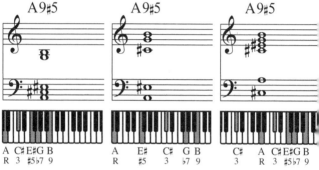

A9♯5

A C♯ E♯ G B
R 3 ♯5 ♭7 9

A9♯5

A E♯ C♯ G B
R ♯5 3 ♭7 9

A9♯5

C♯ A C♯ E♯ G B
3 R 3 ♯5 ♭7 9

Major Ninth (maj9, M9, ma9, 9) [R–3–5–7–9]

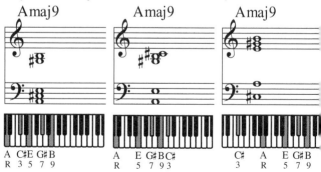

Amaj9

A C♯ E G♯ B
R 3 5 7 9

Amaj9

A E G♯ B C♯
R 5 7 9 3

Amaj9

C♯ A E G♯ B
3 R 5 7 9

A

Minor Ninth (m9, min9, -9) [R–♭3–5–♭7–9]

Am9

A C E G B
R ♭3 5 ♭7 9

Am9

A E C G B
R 5 ♭3 ♭7 9

Am9

C A E G B
♭3 R 5 ♭7 9

Eleventh Chords

Minor-Major Ninth
[m(maj9), m/M9]
[R–♭3–5–7–9]

Am(maj9)

A E B C G♯
R 5 9 ♭3 7

Dominant Eleventh
(11) [R–5–♭7–9–11]

A11

A E G B D
R 5 ♭7 9 11

Minor Eleventh
(m11, min11, -11)
[R–♭3–5–♭7–9–11]

Am11

A E B D E G C
R 5 9 11 5 ♭7 ♭3

A

Thirteenth Chords

Dominant Thirteenth
(13) [R–3–5–♭7–9–13]

Major Thirteenth
(maj13, M13, ma13)
[R–3–5–7–9–13]

Minor Thirteenth
(m13, min13, -13)
[R–♭3–5–♭7–9–11–13]

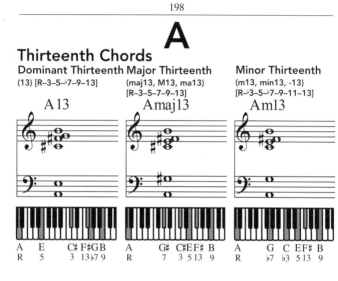

Sixth Chords

Sixth Chords (6) [R–3–5–6]

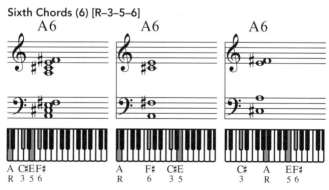

A

Six-Nine Chords ($^6_9$) [R–3–5–6–9]

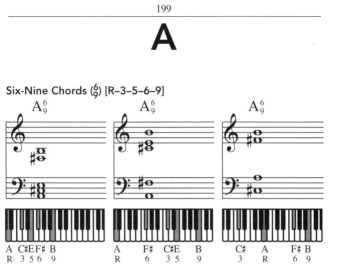

A^6_9 — A C#E F# B / R 3 5 6 9

A^6_9 — A F# C#E B / R 6 3 5 9

A^6_9 — C# A F# B / 3 R 6 9

Minor Sixth Chords (m6) [R–♭3–5–6]

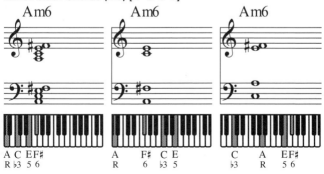

Am6 — A C E F# / R ♭3 5 6

Am6 — A F# C E / R 6 ♭3 5

Am6 — C A E F# / ♭3 R 5 6

A

Minor Six-Nine Chords (m⁶₉) [R–♭3–5–6–9]

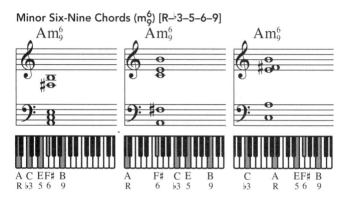

Power Chords ("5" Chords) [R–5]

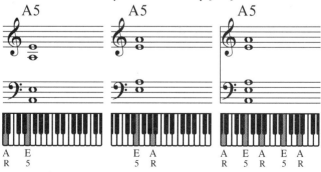

A

Suspended (sus) and add Chords

Sus2 [R–2–5]

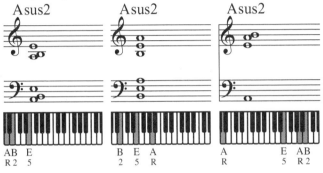

Sus4 [R–4–5]

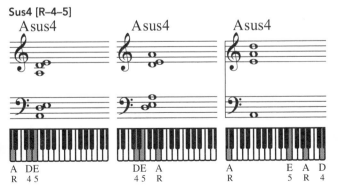

A

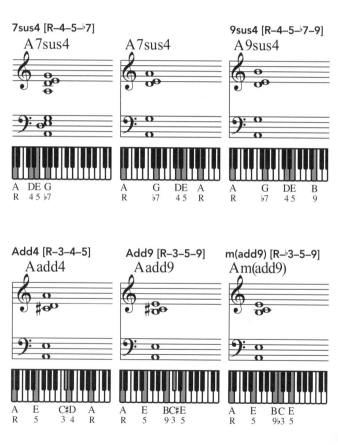

7sus4 [R–4–5–♭7]
A7sus4

A7sus4

9sus4 [R–4–5–♭7–9]
A9sus4

Add4 [R–3–4–5]
Aadd4

Add9 [R–3–5–9]
Aadd9

m(add9) [R–♭3–5–9]
Am(add9)

A♯/B♭

Triads

Major [R–3–5]

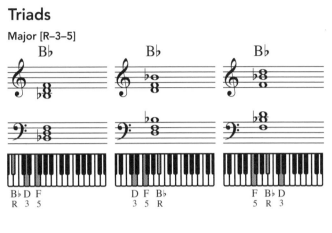

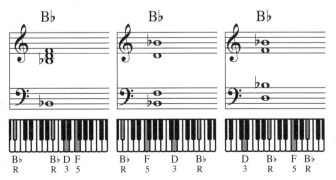

A♯/B♭

Minor (m, -) [R–♭3–5]

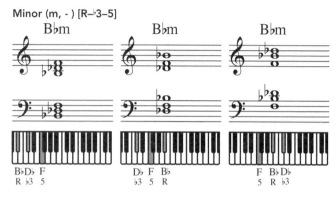

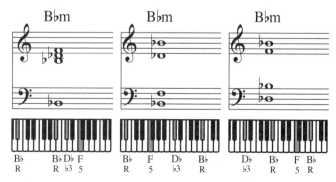

A♯/B♭

Diminished (°, dim) [R–♭3–♭5]

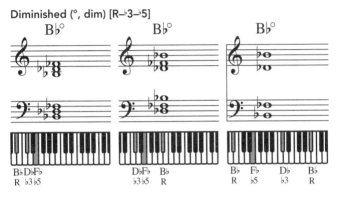

Augmented (+, aug) [R–3–♯5]

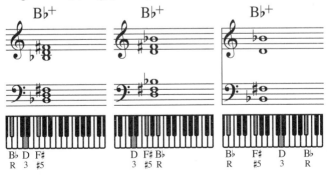

A♯/B♭

Seventh Chords

Dominant Seventh (7) [R–3–5–♭7]

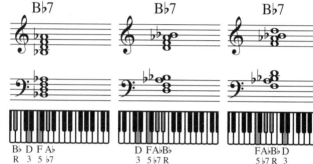

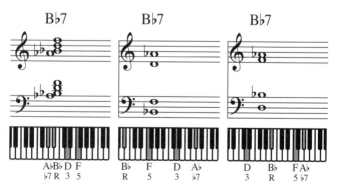

A♯/B♭

Dominant Seventh Chords with Alterations

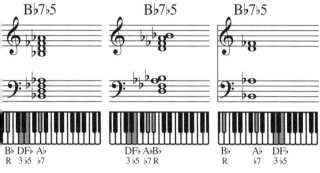

B♭7♭5

B♭7♭5

B♭7♭5

B♭ DF♭ A♭
R 3 ♭5 ♭7

DF♭ A♭B♭
3 ♭5 ♭7 R

B♭   A♭   DF♭
R   ♭7   3 ♭5

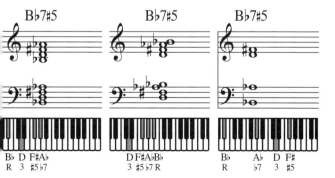

B♭7♯5

B♭7♯5

B♭7♯5

B♭ D F♯A♭
R 3 ♯5 ♭7

D F♯A♭B♭
3 ♯5 ♭7 R

B♭   A♭   D F♯
R   ♭7   3 ♯5

A♯/B♭

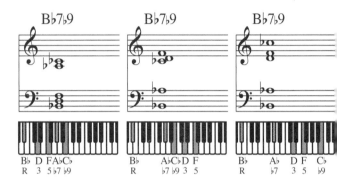

B♭7♭9	B♭7♭9	B♭7♭9

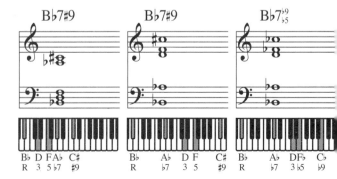

B♭7♯9	B♭7♯9	B♭7♭9♭5

A♯/B♭

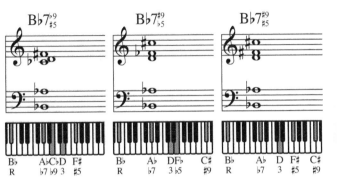

$B♭7^{♭9}_{♯5}$

Bb   AbCbD   F#
R   b7 b9 3   #5

$B♭7^{♯9}_{♭5}$

Bb   Ab   DFb   C#
R   b7   3 b5   #9

$B♭7^{♯9}_{♯5}$

Bb   Ab   D   F#   C#
R   b7   3   #5   #9

Major Seventh (maj7, M7, ma7, 7) [R–3–5–7]

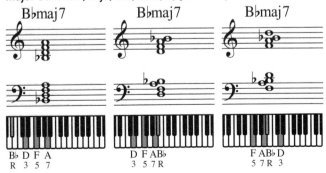

Bbmaj7

Bb D F A
R 3 5 7

Bbmaj7

D F ABb
3 5 7 R

Bbmaj7

F ABb D
5 7 R 3

A♯/B♭

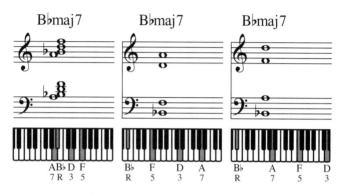

B♭maj7

AB♭ D F
7 R 3 5

B♭maj7

B♭ F D A
R 5 3 7

B♭maj7

B♭ A F D
R 7 5 3

Major Seventh Chords with Alterations

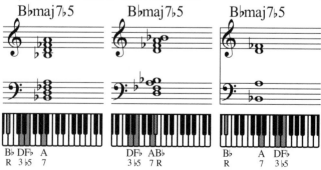

B♭maj7♭5

B♭ DF♭ A
R 3♭5 7

B♭maj7♭5

DF♭ AB♭
3♭5 7 R

B♭maj7♭5

B♭ A DF♭
R 7 3♭5

A#/Bb

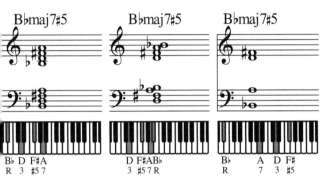

Bbmaj7#5	Bbmaj7#5	Bbmaj7#5
Bb D F#A	D F#ABb	Bb A D F#
R 3 #5 7	3 #5 7 R	R 7 3 #5

Minor Seventh (m7, min7, -7) [R–b3–5–b7]

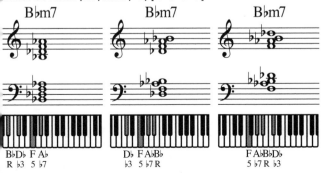

Bbm7	Bbm7	Bbm7
Bb Db F Ab	Db F Ab Bb	F Ab Bb Db
R b3 5 b7	b3 5 b7 R	5 b7 R b3

A♯/B♭

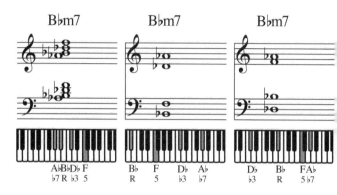

B♭m7

A♭B♭D♭ F
♭7 R ♭3 5

B♭m7

B♭   F   D♭ A♭
R   5   ♭3 ♭7

B♭m7

D♭   B♭   FA♭
♭3   R   5 ♭7

Minor Seventh Chords with Alterations

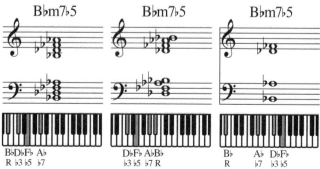

B♭m7♭5

B♭D♭F♭ A♭
R ♭3 ♭5 ♭7

B♭m7♭5

D♭F♭ A♭B♭
♭3 ♭5 ♭7 R

B♭m7♭5

B♭   A♭   D♭F♭
R   ♭7   ♭3 ♭5

A♯/B♭

Minor-Major Seventh [m(maj7), m/M7] [R–♭3–5–7]

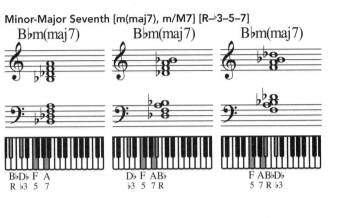

B♭m(maj7) B♭m(maj7) B♭m(maj7)

B♭ D♭ F A D♭ F A B♭ F A B♭ D♭
R ♭3 5 7   ♭3 5 7 R   5 7 R ♭3

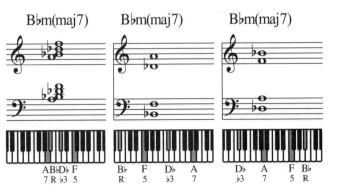

B♭m(maj7) B♭m(maj7) B♭m(maj7)

A B♭ D♭ F B♭ F D♭ A D♭ A F B♭
7 R ♭3 5   R   5 ♭3 7 ♭3 7 5 R

A♯/B♭

Diminished Seventh (°7) [R–♭3–♭5–♭♭7]

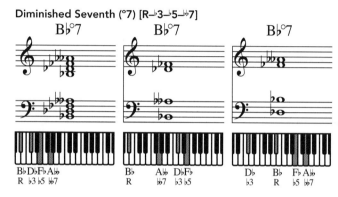

Ninth Chords

Dominant Ninth (9) [R–3–5–♭7–9]

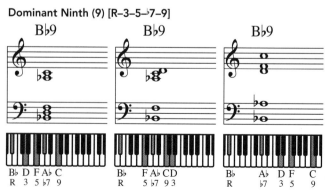

A♯/B♭

Dominant Ninth Chords with Alterations

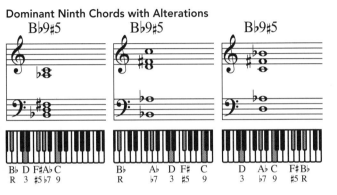

Bb9#5 — Bb D F#Ab C / R 3 #5 b7 9

Bb9#5 — Bb Ab D F# C / R b7 3 #5 9

Bb9#5 — D Ab C F# Bb / 3 b7 9 #5 R

Major Ninth (maj9, M9, ma9, 9) [R–3–5–7–9]

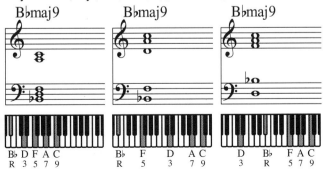

Bbmaj9 — Bb D F A C / R 3 5 7 9

Bbmaj9 — Bb F D A C / R 5 3 7 9

Bbmaj9 — D Bb F A C / 3 R 5 7 9

A#/B♭

Minor Ninth (m9, min9, -9) [R–♭3–5–♭7–9]

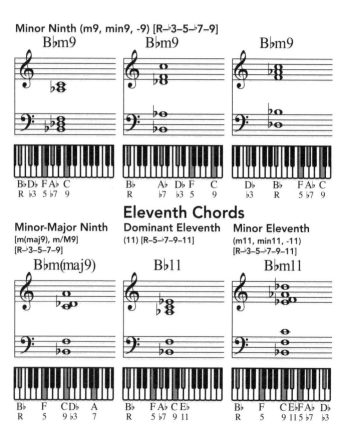

B♭m9

B♭m9

B♭m9

B♭	D♭	F	A♭	C
R	♭3	5	♭7	9

B♭	A♭	D♭	F	C
R	♭7	♭3	5	9

D♭	B♭	F	A♭	C
♭3	R	5	♭7	9

Eleventh Chords

Minor-Major Ninth
[m(maj9), m/M9]
[R–♭3–5–7–9]

Dominant Eleventh
(11) [R–5–♭7–9–11]

Minor Eleventh
(m11, min11, -11)
[R–♭3–5–♭7–9–11]

B♭m(maj9)

B♭11

B♭m11

B♭	F	C	D♭	A
R	5	9	♭3	7

B♭	F	A♭	C	E♭
R	5	♭7	9	11

B♭	F	C	E♭	F	A♭	D♭
R	5	9	11	5	♭7	♭3

A#/B♭

Thirteenth Chords

Dominant Thirteenth
(13) [R–3–5–♭7–9–13]

Major Thirteenth
(maj13, M13, ma13)
[R–3–5–7–9–13]

Minor Thirteenth
(m13, min13, -13)
[R–♭3–5–♭7–9–11–13]

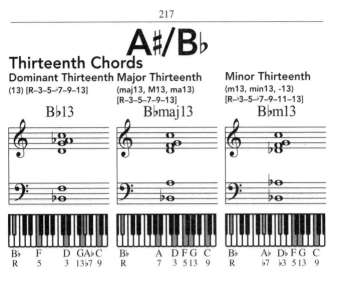

B♭13 — B♭ F D G A♭ C / R 5 3 13 ♭7 9

B♭maj13 — B♭ A D F G C / R 7 3 5 13 9

B♭m13 — B♭ A♭ D♭ F G C / R ♭7 ♭3 5 13 9

Sixth Chords

Sixth Chords (6) [R–3–5–6]

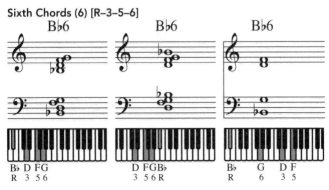

B♭6 — B♭ D F G / R 3 5 6

B♭6 — D F G B♭ / 3 5 6 R

B♭6 — B♭ G D F / R 6 3 5

A♯/B♭

Six-Nine Chords (⁶⁄₉) [R–3–5–6–9]

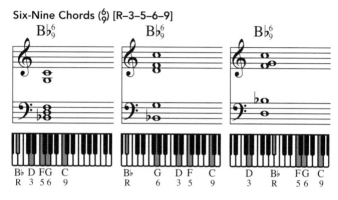

Minor Sixth Chords (m6) [R–♭3–5–6]

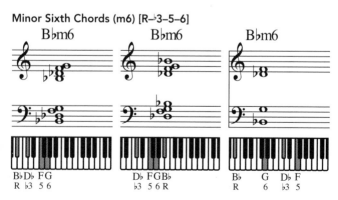

A♯/B♭

Minor Six-Nine Chords (m$_9^6$) [R–♭3–5–6–9]

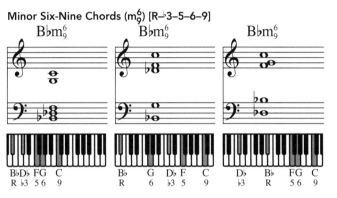

B♭m$_9^6$ B♭m$_9^6$ B♭m$_9^6$

B♭	D♭	F	G	C
R	♭3	5	6	9

B♭	G	D♭	F	C
R	6	♭3	5	9

D♭	B♭	F	G	C
♭3	R	5	6	9

Power Chords ("5" Chords) [R–5]

B♭5   B♭5   B♭5

B♭	F
R	5

F	B♭
5	R

B♭	F	B♭	F	B♭
R	5	R	5	R

A♯/B♭

Suspended (sus) and add Chords

Sus2 [R–2–5]

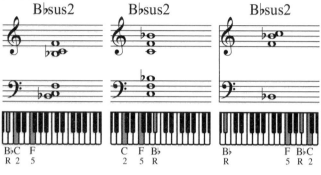

Bbsus2   Bbsus2   Bbsus2

B♭C F   C F B♭   B♭ F B♭C
R 2 5   2 5 R   R 5 R 2

Sus4 [R–4–5]

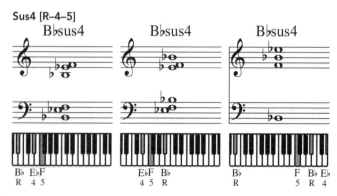

Bbsus4   Bbsus4   Bbsus4

B♭ E♭F   E♭F B♭   B♭ F B♭ E♭
R 4 5   4 5 R   R 5 R 4

A♯/B♭

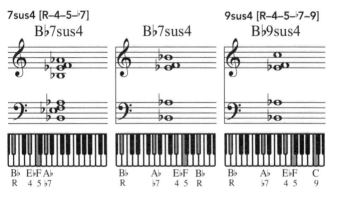

7sus4 [R–4–5–♭7]
Bb7sus4

Bb7sus4

9sus4 [R–4–5–♭7–9]
Bb9sus4

Bb	Eb F Ab
R	4 5 ♭7

Bb	Ab	Eb F	Bb
R	♭7	4 5	R

Bb	Ab	Eb F	C
R	♭7	4 5	9

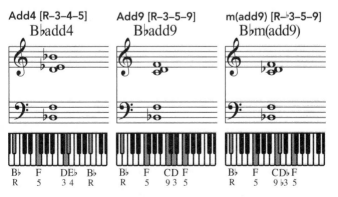

Add4 [R–3–4–5]
Bbadd4

Add9 [R–3–5–9]
Bbadd9

m(add9) [R–♭3–5–9]
Bbm(add9)

Bb	F	DEb	Bb
R	5	3 4	R

Bb	F	CD	F
R	5	9 3	5

Bb	F	CDb	F
R	5	9 ♭3	5

B

Triads

Major [R–3–5]

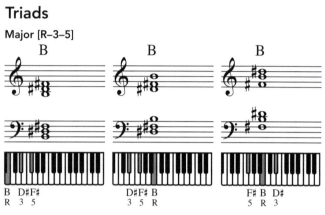

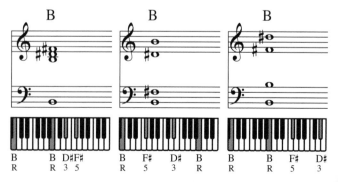

B

Minor (m, -) [R–♭3–5]

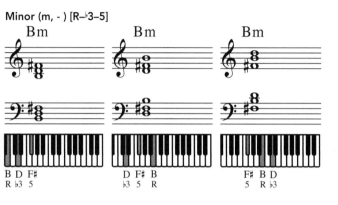

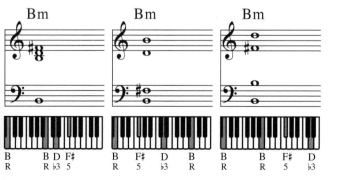

B

Diminished (°, dim) [R–♭3–♭5]

Augmented (+, aug) [R–3–♯5]

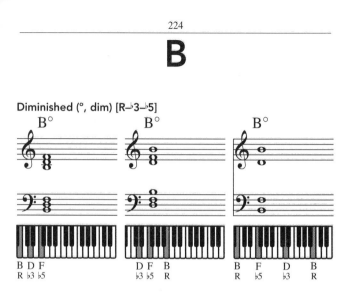

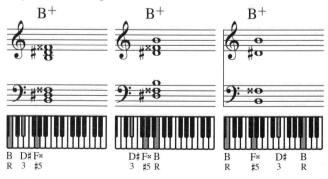

B

Seventh Chords

Dominant Seventh (7) [R–3–5–♭7]

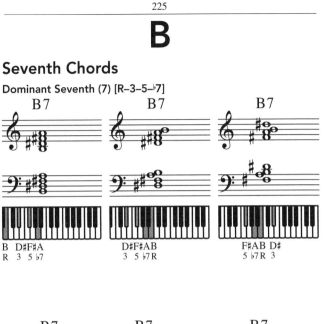

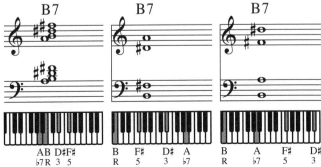

B

Dominant Seventh Chords with Alterations

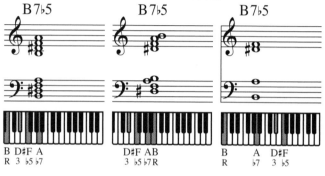

B 7♭5	B 7♭5	B 7♭5
B D#F A	D#F AB	B A D#F
R 3 ♭5 ♭7	3 ♭5 ♭7 R	R ♭7 3 ♭5

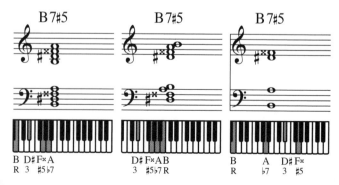

B 7#5	B 7#5	B 7#5
B D#F×A	D#F×AB	B A D# F×
R 3 #5 ♭7	3 #5 ♭7 R	R ♭7 3 #5

B

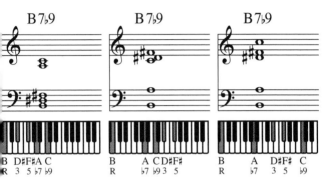

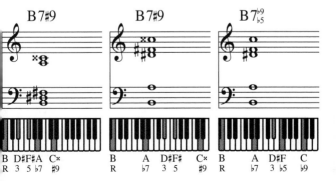

B

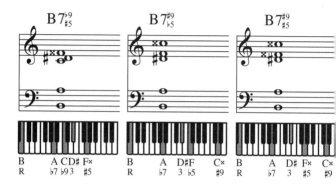

$B7^{\flat9}_{\#5}$ · $B7^{\#9}_{\flat5}$ · $B7^{\#9}_{\#5}$

B	A	C	D#	F×	
R	♭7	♭9	3		#5

B	A	D#	F	C×
R	♭7	3	♭5	#9

B	A	D#	F×	C×
R	♭7	3	#5	#9

Major Seventh (maj7, M7, ma7, 7) [R–3–5–7]

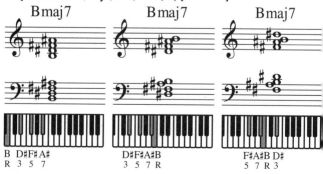

Bmaj7 · Bmaj7 · Bmaj7

B	D#	F#	A#
R	3	5	7

D#	F#	A#	B
3	5	7	R

F#	A#	B	D#
5	7	R	3

B

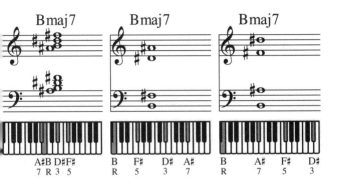

Bmaj7   Bmaj7   Bmaj7

A#B D#F#   B   F#   D#   A#   B   A#   F#   D#
7 R 3 5   R   5   3   7   R   7   5   3

Major Seventh Chords with Alterations

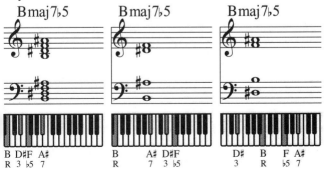

Bmaj7♭5   Bmaj7♭5   Bmaj7♭5

B D#F A#   B   A# D#F   D#   B   F A#
R 3 ♭5 7   R   7   3 ♭5   3   R   ♭5 7

B

Bmaj7#5   Bmaj7#5   Bmaj7#5

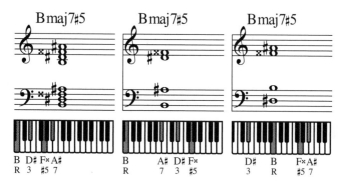

B D# F× A#
R 3 #5 7

B   A# D# F×
R   7   3 #5

D# B   F× A#
3   R   #5 7

Minor Seventh (m7, min7, -7) [R–♭3–5–♭7]

Bm7   Bm7   Bm7

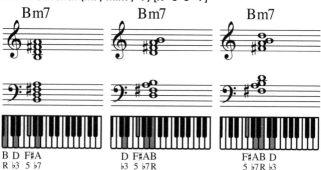

B D F#A
R ♭3 5 ♭7

D F#AB
♭3 5 ♭7R

F#AB D
5 ♭7R ♭3

B

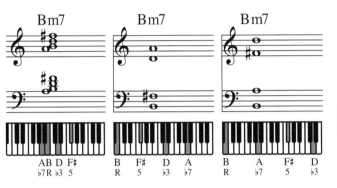

Bm7   Bm7   Bm7

Minor Seventh Chords with Alterations

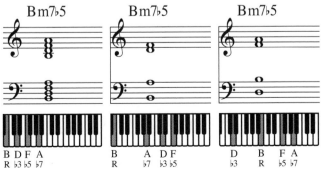

Bm7♭5   Bm7♭5   Bm7♭5

B

Minor-Major Seventh [m(maj7), m/M7] [R–♭3–5–7]

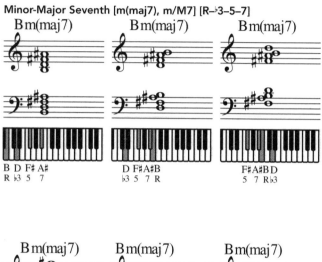

Bm(maj7)
B D F# A#
R ♭3 5 7

Bm(maj7)
D F#A#B
♭3 5 7 R

Bm(maj7)
F#A#B D
5 7 R♭3

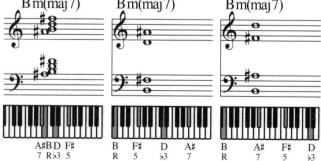

Bm(maj7)
A#B D F#
7 R♭3 5

Bm(maj7)
B F# D A#
R 5 ♭3 7

Bm(maj7)
B A# F# D
R 7 5 ♭3

B

Diminished Seventh (°7) [R–♭3–♭5–♭♭7]

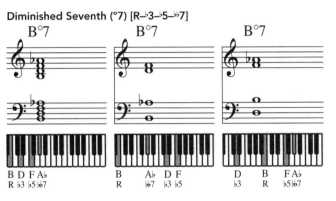

Ninth Chords

Dominant Ninth (9) [R–3–5–♭7–9]

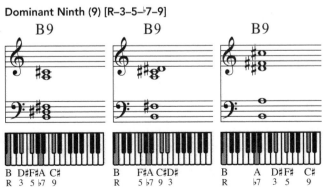

B

Dominant Ninth Chords with Alterations

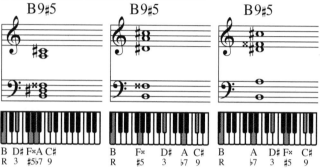

B9♯5   B9♯5   B9♯5

B	D♯	F×	A	C♯
R	3	♯5	♭7	9

B		F×	D♯	A	C♯
R		♯5	3	♭7	9

B		A	D♯	F×	C♯
R		♭7	3	♯5	9

Major Ninth (maj9, M9, ma9, 9) [R–3–5–7–9]

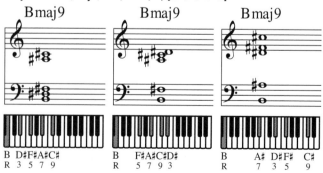

Bmaj9   Bmaj9   Bmaj9

B	D♯	F♯	A♯	C♯
R	3	5	7	9

B		F♯	A♯	C♯	D♯
R		5	7	9	3

B		A♯	D♯	F♯	C♯
R		7	3	5	9

B

Minor Ninth (m9, min9, -9) [R–♭3–5–♭7–9]

Bm9

B D F#A C#
R ♭3 5 ♭7 9

Bm9

B F# D A C#
R 5 ♭3 ♭7 9

Bm9

B A D F# C#
R ♭7 ♭3 5 9

Eleventh Chords

Minor-Major Ninth
[m(maj9), m/M9]
[R–♭3–5–7–9]

Bm(maj9)

B F# C#D A#
R 5 9 ♭3 7

Dominant Eleventh
(11) [R–5–♭7–9–11]

B 11

B F#A C# E
R 5 ♭7 9 11

Minor Eleventh
(m11, min11, -11)
[R–♭3–5–♭7–9–11]

Bm11

B F# C#EF#A D
R 5 9 115 ♭7 ♭3

B

Thirteenth Chords

Dominant Thirteenth
(13) [R–3–5–♭7–9–13]

Major Thirteenth
(maj13, M13, ma13)
[R–3–5–7–9–13]

Minor Thirteenth
(m13, min13, -13)
[R–♭3–5–♭7–9–11–13]

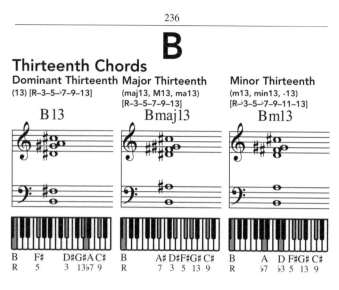

Sixth Chords

Sixth Chords (6) [R–3–5–6]

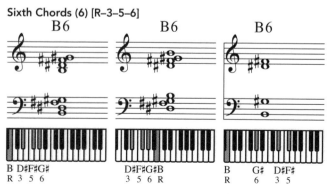

B

Six-Nine Chords ($^6_9$) [R–3–5–6–9]

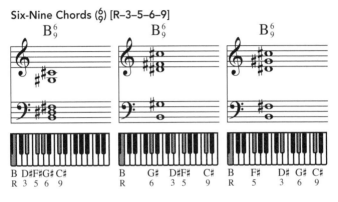

Minor Sixth Chords (m6) [R–♭3–5–6]

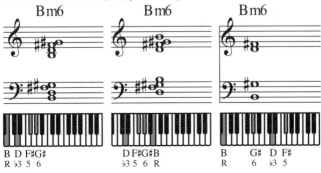

Minor Six-Nine Chords (m⁶₉) [R–♭3–5–6–9]

Power Chords ("5" Chords) [R–5]

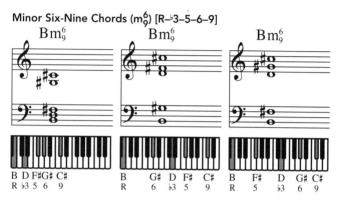

B

Suspended (sus) and add Chords

Sus2 [R–2–5]

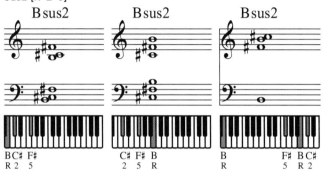

Sus4 [R–4–5]

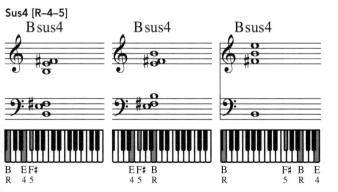

B

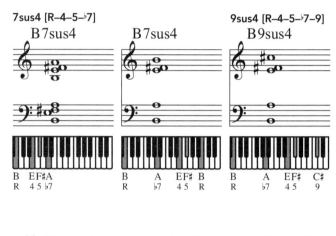

7sus4 [R–4–5–♭7]

B7sus4

B7sus4

9sus4 [R–4–5–♭7–9]

B9sus4

B	EF#A		B	A	EF#	B	B	A	EF#	C#
R	4 5 ♭7		R	♭7	4 5	R	R	♭7	4 5	9

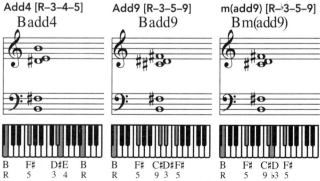

Add4 [R–3–4–5]

Badd4

Add9 [R–3–5–9]

Badd9

m(add9) [R–♭3–5–9]

Bm(add9)

B	F#	D#E	B	B	F#	C#D#F#	B	F#	C#D	F#
R	5	3 4	R	R	5	9 3 5	R	5	9 ♭3	5